T0158812

MISUSED

Revealing the Fact, Faith, and Truth of Biblical Encouragement

R. K. AYERS

WESTBOW
PRESS®
A DIVISION OF THOMAS NELSON
& ZONDERVAN

WestBow Press books may be ordered through booksellers or by contacting:

WestBow Press
A Division of Thomas Nelson & Zondervan
1663 Liberty Drive
Bloomington, IN 47403
www.westbowpress.com
1 (866) 928-1240

ISBN: 978-1-5127-5040-9 (sc)
ISBN: 978-1-5127-5042-3 (hc)
ISBN: 978-1-5127-5041-6 (e)

Library of Congress Control Number: 2016912839

Print information available on the last page.

WestBow Press rev. date: 8/11/2016

To Thu-Thao and the boys for allowing me the countless hours to write

CONTENTS

I am a chaplain with a passion for counseling. They say confession is good for the soul, and in that is my confession. While so many people expect chaplains to be great teachers and theologians, I simply love to spend time encouraging people in the midst of their struggles and pain. This encouragement can mean that I point them toward Christ or help them understand why bad situations have entered into their lives. Regardless, chaplaincy and counseling go hand in hand.

The unfortunate part is that so many people believe that biblically based counseling—or Christian counseling—in mainstream psychology is the witty ability to make pithy faith-based statements they might have heard from someone else. I have seen and heard it time and time again. Counselors and faith leaders make statements that just are not used in the right context.

Their hearts are in the right place. I know they are trying to point someone to the hope found in Christ, but really they are pointing down a wrong path that might or might not lead to Christ. As a chaplain, I want to see changed spiritual lives, and as a counselor, I want to see changed emotional lives. I have a feeling there are not many people of the Christian faith who desire something different. However, in their desire to help people, they pull what I call "canned Christian comments" out of their mind with a hope that it will make them and other people feel better.

When I hear people make statements like "God will never give you more than you can handle" or "God makes everything happen for good," it makes me cringe. So many Bible verses are taken out of context or even misused that it saddens me. Some of the verses make complete sense when used correctly, but others just don't apply to the intended situation.

Working in a hospital environment, I have heard people make these comments as a means to encourage multiple areas of their lives. The biggest question is, why do people say things that are not true or that do not apply to the situation? This question must be addressed, as our society has lost its way in effectively guiding others toward the truth found in Christ.

As I write this book, in no way am I claiming that I have never used any of these statements myself at times of frustration and desperation to help someone get through a difficult situation. When I hear the words come out of my mouth, I always want to kick myself for even uttering them. I know better, and in the long run, every Christian should know better.

Now, before we go further, this might be a good time for me to let you know that I will step on your toes. This book is designed to help you understand what we are against in the world, not what makes you feel good about how you are living your Christian life. There will be statements that might offend you, but you must ask yourself, "Am I offended because I resemble the statement, or am I offended because I made the statement?"

If you resemble the statement, let me encourage you to make a change in your life that points toward a deeper, knowing relationship with God, one that cannot be wavered by the misuse of scripture or the manipulation of theology by people who just want to make us feel better about ourselves.

If you are offended because I made the statement, please know that it is made not in anger but in frustration. Hypocritical thinking and straying away from the truth of scripture is causing the apathy that our Christian culture is facing today. I only make bold and sometimes blunt statements in an attitude of love—a love for God and His people. We are all commissioned to teach the Bible in truth and spirit.

As a result, I have written this book to help people understand why they say what they say and what they should be able to say. Before we get into the real work, let's look at why people even say things that are not true or out of context. There are three primary reasons I believe people make these statements. All three are based on the influences—or lack of—in their lives.

1. Some who make the statement simply do not know the truth. It would be irresponsible of me to think that people who use

faith-based encouragement know the truth. Many people, even those sitting in pews today, do not know the truth. Some have never opened a Bible or, in today's society, opened their Bible app on an electronic device. Simply put, there are those who are lost in the middle of their church, some by the fault of the church and others by their own fault. When they depend solely on the church for their understanding of God, they will hear truth but will not understand what the truth really is because their understanding of truth is limited to Sunday-morning services. Unfortunately most are scanning social media or trying to catch the pastor in wrong interpretation by fact-checking on popular search engines. The truth is something learned when we talk about the scripture. Without truth, we are simply giving opinion. As a college professor, I often critique my students on their lack of citations or references. I have had students speak to issues that could only be based in opinion because if they would simply research the subject, they would find their statement to be inaccurate. In the same respect, people innocently make inaccurate statements based on opinion because they have failed to open their Bibles for themselves and learn to understand God and His Word at a deeper level.

2. People make the statements they do because it is what they have always heard. Understand that every one of these statements used in the right context is helpful. The unfortunate part is that we have not really learned what the right context is. We grow up hearing statements like "turn the other cheek" or "the truth will set you free." Almost all the statements in this book are verbatim from the Bible itself. When you look at the verses before and after them, you will see they are misused to manipulate various situations. When I was young, a bully at school wanted to fight me. When I told my dad, he gave me the advice to show love toward him and treat him with respect. And then he would change his ways. This is great advice, but it was very aggravating when he would knock the books out of my hand, push me around, or encourage the other kids to alienate me on the playground. Before we go further, this was a time when bullying was not in the forefront of educators' minds.

This was when you showed leadership and maturity by handling your problems unless they were life threatening. At that time, even telling the teacher resulted in advice versus action. So when I showed the bully respect and compassion, he walked all over me. He treated me as if I were his servant. He would try to make me do things I did not want to do, so finally I told him to meet me at the corner of the school and we would solve the problem with a fight. I am sure it came out differently, but the challenge was on. After school, I made my way to the corner, along with some of the other kids in the school who'd heard of the challenge. I stood on that corner waiting, nervous, excited, and downright scared of what this kid might do to me. I couldn't show it in front of the other kids though. Fifteen minutes and then thirty minutes passed. After forty-five minutes, there was still no bully. He did not show. I do not know why he did not come, but after that, he did not push me around, and while we had a mutual respect for each other, there was an understanding that I would not bow to his every whim. This is not to say that we should solve all our problems as Christians by fighting. I am saying that we are often told to turn the other cheek. Eventually we become pushovers. This book is also a call for Christians to stand up for what they believe, speak in truth, and stop regurgitating statements that might or might not work. When we look at statements that are said because that is what we have always heard, over time the translation becomes more distorted and misused. As Christians it is not our job to regurgitate these statements, but it is our duty to know what to say, when to say it, and how it appropriately applies to the circumstances we are in.

3. Many people do not know what to say in stressful circumstances, but they want to make themselves feel better in the situation. Unfortunately this is the most common one. People want to feel better about themselves. They want to know that what they are saying might have helped someone. Even more, because they are uncomfortable in their situation, they want to feel as if what they are saying has helped them. When I was working as a medical

chaplain, I had just finished sitting in a meeting with a family. The doctors were telling the family their loved one was in the last stages of life. This family was going to lose their daughter, wife, mother, and friend. She was just one person, but held different meanings to every loved one in the waiting room ready to hear the results of the meeting. As we sat in the room, I sat quietly as usual, waiting for my turn to speak. When the time finally came, everyone in the room turned to me, waiting for some great words of wisdom that might provide encouragement in this sorrowful situation. I simply said, "After we finish here, let's gather with your support network in the waiting room for a time of reflection." It was not what the medical staff expected to hear. I had spent time with this family. I knew them, and I had been providing encouragement throughout their stay at the hospital. However, one young doctor was not satisfied so he closed the session with, "I know these circumstances can be difficult, but in situations like this, God never gives you more than you can handle." I was floored. First, the doctor making the statement was agnostic. I knew this because the medical professional's position was made clear to me during other visits to the floor. However, because the doctor did not know what to say to close the conversation and was feeling bad about the news that had just been given to the family, this statement was inaccurate yet encouraged the doctor was made.

We do this all the time. In fact, it is so common that we try to make ourselves feel better that many of us have developed misused statements as part of our normal speech when people tell us something discouraging or we are facing trials ourselves. Ultimately they become cliché and lose their meaning when it really matters.

This is yet another reason I wrote this book. People need to understand what they are saying in the name of the Lord. If you do not make these statements, this book still might help you understand the world around you. I have set up this book for multiple uses, and it will help every reader understand the misuse of these scriptures or sayings.

I have broken down each chapter into sections that can be taught as lessons in a small group or for individual spiritual growth:

1. The first part of the chapter will speak to the statement itself and how society—both secular and Christian—misuse the statement. In this first section, the Bible verses most associated with the statement will be given.

2. The second section of the chapter focuses on the context of the misused verses. This context is based on the verses before and after the misused verse, along with understanding what applications these verses provide for the Christian life. In the same respect, it will speak to why society might misuse the verse and why it is improperly used.

3. The third section is designed to help readers understand what should be used instead. In all my leadership and military training, I have learned that you never thoroughly discuss a problem without having some solution, and that is what this section is specifically designed for. I am not going to tell you something is wrong without helping you find a better solution.

4. The chapter ends with questions that are designed for personal or group reflection. This is to help you get your mind moving in the right direction for personal growth. However, this is not designed to be a self-help book. It is set up to be a personal change book, something that inspires change in the way you help others. This is structured to help you be a better encourager, minister, and brother or sister in Christ.

If you are using this book for personal spiritual growth, I encourage you spend time with the questions in the back after reading each chapter. I have designed this book to read like a devotional that brings light to situations our society faces every day. Take each chapter one at a time, learn from it, and grow from it.

If you are using this book as a small group resource, it is best to have each person read the chapter between meetings. When you reconvene at your next gathering, discuss the chapter and answer the questions at the end of each chapter. The questions are designed to spark conversation, so if the small group discusses the chapter without using the questions, it is okay. That being said, you know your small group better than I do, so if there are other questions, feel free to add those too.

Finally, if you are using this book to have a better understanding of how to help the hurting, this resource can help redirect and even direct others through difficult situations in their lives. Feel free to use the resources as you see fit. The questions in the back can help you guide counseling sessions and help those you are assisting understand the dynamic of their situation.

As stated before, I am a chaplain and counselor. By the nature of the business, I have experienced a great deal of trials and traumas in people's lives. In this book, you will see my understanding of these statements from both experience and studied knowledge. All the names, locations, and some of the situations in this book have been changed to protect confidentiality and privileged communication. Any examples that reflect real-life people, names, or situations are merely coincidence.

I pray and hope this book brings understanding and clarity in the midst of your struggles as well as helping others understand how God can bring them through their struggles.

SESSION 1: WHY THE BIBLE?

Within the covers of the Bible are the answers for all the problems men face.

—Ronald Reagan, fortieth president
of the United States

When I was a young youth pastor, I encountered something that seemed unusual at the time, but as my experience progressed, I found it to be more common than I had originally thought.

A boy came to youth group with a Bible in his pocket, and he began to show this Bible to all the kids, stating, "This is my guidebook." His Bible held just as much truth as anything we would read from in the teaching time that night. Shortly after showing some of the youth his guidebook, they began to come to me with complaints about what he was showing them. His Bible was a Satanic book of worship.

The boy's declaration of the truth in his text created a big stir in the youth group that night. Sensing the uncomfortable stir among the youth before the group started signaled me to talk with the young boy. He lived locally and was the only one in his family that dawned the doors of a church, which made the conversation even more sensitive because, depending on what I said and how I confronted the issue, the results could be glorious or disastrous. So I pulled him aside and asked about the book he was showing everyone. Scared and worried, he pushed me and ran out the door toward his home. The young boy did come back a few minutes later, without his Satanic book of worship.

Experiences like these make people ask why the Bible is so important as the foundational book of Christian living. That night in youth group, I was challenged with many questions about all the books people put their faith in or even why the Holy Bible is the truth of what the Christian faith believes. At the time, the only answer I could give was that people put faith in another sacred text other than the Bible because of social saturation that creates confusion for people who are looking for answers to their personal strife and overwhelming stressors in life.

As I matured in personal faith and did more research, I found there are nineteen major religions broke down into two hundred and seventy classifications and more than thirty-four thousand forms of Christianity in the world today. More so, there are twenty-five hundred recognized gods in the world today. It is believed that more than 320 million entities are prayed to or depended on for power, direction, and wisdom. If this didn't confuse people enough as it is, people searching for spirituality can choose from nearly thirty texts that will supposedly give them direction and purpose on their faith journey.

There is no wonder our society is confused about religion. Each of those texts give principles on how people should live, quality and value for life, as well as some false teachings that display a disregard for humanity as a means of spiritual advancement. When people are in the midst of spiritual crisis, a search takes place. They want something that will work for them and develop their inner confidence—the hope to know, in the midst of their weakness, something greater than themselves has control over their situation.

To have the confidence that something greater than us has control over life's situations can only come from a place of faith. If people are convincing enough, others will follow and believe, regardless of what is required of them or how crazy the notion might be. While many naysayers might not respect the Bible for its value, both historically and spiritually, many other religious beliefs, spiritual philosophy, and theology comes from concepts developed in the Bible.

The Bible is more complex than a book you read from cover to cover. People should understand what the Bible says, know how to read it, and learn where to look for historical parallels. When this happens, they become aware of the truths found in it. This means that people of the Christian faith can speak with confidence that the Holy Bible is God's truth based on the Holy Spirit's prompting. When we speak with the power of God's Word, as God intended, there is no doubt those who believe will find encouragement, growth, and sustainment through any and every trial they face in the world today.

Simply put, Christians believe in one God-inspired text because the Holy Spirit serves as their counselor through all time and works in everyone's lives at different levels and circumstances based on spiritual maturity and preparation. The one God-inspired text known as the Holy Bible is essential for Christians because it is God's Word through His people in all situations until the end of time, not just in the moment it was written.

Through the pages of the Bible, we can see the development of the Jewish faith, God's law under Abrahamic and Mosaic covenant, and the redemption of His people through the new covenant. Moreover, through the Bible, people can see that salvation is open to everyone: Jew, Gentile, sinner, and favored. Unlike many other religions, the only conditions are based on confessing with your mouth and believing in your heart (Rom. 10:9), as well as love of God and others (Luke 10:27). Many of the other aspects of Christianity are not mandatory for salvation but essential for spiritual growth and a relationship with God.

The issue modern Christianity faces today is common to the church throughout history: preferred theology and inaccurate interpretation. Paul faced these issues as he worked to guide and establish the first-century church. While he was telling people about the simple requirements to receive God's grace, a group of people traveled behind him, adding other conditions. They were telling the new Christians and those seeking a relationship with God through Jesus that they must follow additional laws to truly be saved. And these additional laws caused Paul to write a letter to Timothy, ensuring he was aware of two specific things regarding ministering to people (2 Tim. 3:13–17):

1. He needed to be aware of false teachers. This is something Paul battled his entire ministry. Timothy was warned against it, and more, it is something we battle in our spiritual lives today.

2. He instructed him to understand how the scriptures are profitable for ministry. By the time Paul wrote Timothy letters of instruction

for ministerial leadership, many of Paul's letters were circulating through the churches. It was important because these letters were not only instruction but also encouragement in the midst of Roman oppression and persecution.

As we look at these verses, it can become apparent that believers today face the same confusion, false teaching, misunderstanding of God's Word, and oppressive systems. Paul's warning and instruction to Timothy is the same we as Christian's today should be aware of in our own walk. Most importantly we have to understand that false teachers are everywhere.

IDENTIFYING THE FALSE TEACHER

I have encountered many people in my career who claim to be proclaimers of the Gospel. These people, with a great deal of training, have completely taken the Word of God out of context, misguided others for personal gain, taught people that some sin issues are unforgivable, and ultimately created a stopping block for a personal relationship with God.

I was working with a young couple who was planning to get married and cohabitating. Both were new believers learning about what it meant to be true followers of Christ. In that moment, they were very impressionable when it came to understanding the Christian faith. While I was providing their premarital preparation, they were trying to find a church that really ministered to them and helped them grow in the Word. One particular church they enjoyed attending had missionaries visit for fund-raising and develop cell groups around the city.

The couple, through the advisement of the pastor, invited two young male missionaries to stay with them. The missionaries began to minister to this couple and help them understand the faith at a deeper level. The couple seemed to be benefiting from the missionary teachings, and they were growing in their faith.

Shortly after the missionaries arrived though, one found the woman attractive. When he was with the woman and her fiancé was not home, he would begin flirting with her and giving her extra attention when it came to talking about spiritual growth. Because the conversation was always regarding spirituality, the woman did not recognize what the young man was trying to do.

The conversation started to transition from understanding who God is in their lives to the need to kick her fiancé out of the house because God found their lifestyle a sin. As the trust level grew over the next few days, the missionary fashioned the conversation to convince the woman that she needed to leave him, repent, and start a new relationship because that was what God intended for her. Soon the thin strand of justification from the Bible was turned to claim prophetic words from God. Finally the missionary made bold statements that he was placed in her life because God had told him she was supposed to be with him, not her fiancé.

When her fiancé found out about the issue, I advised him to go to the pastor and tell him what was going on. He listened to the advice, but the pastor advised him that it was not appropriate to challenge a prophetic word from God and to ignore it would be sinful. Both he and his fiancé were mortified! They had been together for more than five years, and now God "wanted" her to leave her fiancé for this other man. Worse yet, the pastor endorsed it. Only after she had kicked her fiancé out of the house, called off the wedding, and attempted to cut all ties with him did he cry out for help.

It is apparent that teachers will tell people things based on their understanding of scripture, but they are not well enough versed in the Word to interpret and develop sound guidance for God's people. False teachers create a great following because they will skew the Bible to fit what people want to hear and not what people oftentimes need to hear. At a greater disadvantage, people will also develop teachings that benefit them and their desire to obtain things for personal gain.

With the couple above, they faced a false teacher who manipulated the Bible in order to obtain something for personal gain. The missionary wanted to be with the woman in the relationship and skewed scriptures to point toward listening to God even when it was inappropriate. The pastor did not investigate a missionary with whom his church was endorsing and misadvised two young Christians trying to do the right thing in God's eyes by getting married. The result could have been disastrous.

By the grace of God, the man and I knew each other long before the missionaries and the pastor came into his life. We immediately began to pray over the situation, and I tried to talk with his fiancée, but the missionary's statements so blinded her that she believed I was misguiding her in defense of my friend. At least that was what the missionary had told her.

Because God answers prayer, a woman at the gym where his fiancée exercised began a conversation with her in a way that she would listen. To make a long story short, through the Holy Spirit moving in the woman at the gym, my friend's fiancé immediately went home and kicked the missionaries out of the house.

The couple continued premarital preparation and were married soon after completion. However, sadly the pastor of the church where the missionaries were based "excommunicated" them and told them they were never welcome there again because they did not listen to God through His people or His Word.

This is what Paul was describing when he was advising Timothy in his second letter. We have to understand there are false teachers in Christian communities that can damage the growth of God's kingdom, both intentionally and unintentionally. Second Timothy 3:13a begins by naming two types of false teachers, evil and impostors. While both types might seem like the same descriptions, they pose very different threats and tactics to manipulate others.

First, we have to look at the similarities between the two. Evil people and imposters have an intentional like-minded attitude to create issues with other people. Unless they are suffering from mental disorders, evil people and imposters search to create problems by enforcing belief systems that present chaos. This is why so many other scriptures and holy texts make sense to those in a desperate search for spiritual, emotional, and physical salvation.

Next, we have to look at the difference between the two. Evil people seek to destroy truth by creating hardships and annoyances. On the other hand, imposters seek to destroy truth by seducing people with lies. The first thing that can be pointed out in this is the intentional destruction of truth. Evil people make an intentional effort to destroy truth.

The destruction of truth can only happen when the lies that are told become believable and gain a following. In order to tell a convincing lie, they have to create hardships and annoyances within the truth, which are not just attempts to create chaos. They are efforts to create issues that are so believable that people can't or won't argue them. This happens because so many believe they don't have the access or intelligence level to research statements for themselves.

We as a society qualify ourselves based on experience and education. I can't count how many times I have heard people say, "He is the pastor. What reason do I have not to believe him?" It is easy to influence people by creating hardships that prevent them from going further. As well, we have no reason to lack trust with those who consider themselves experts in any particular field. What many forget is that evil can be produced out of high levels of experience. There are those who, for whatever reason, take their high level of knowledge and use it for personal gain of money, power, and fame. Those who wish to do evil with knowledge are aware of what is right and wrong. They are well-studied and have great understanding of how to use that knowledge to grow or destroy others through their influence.

Think of an influential person you have ever met in your life. Now take that person's teaching and reflect on the greatest principle he or she taught that influenced your life for positive development. When you do that, it is easy to see how the person you are today was, in part, because of what he or she taught you in life. While it might have been hard for you to become that person and the principle was not easy, it held truth, and your life was impacted because of it.

Now imagine if someone you respected even more came along and told you the principle your other friend taught you was false. The second person knew the first person's statement was true, but for a desire of personal gain, whether it was acceptance, friendship, or money, told you that it was a lie. Because you respected the second person more than the one inserting positive influence, you walked away from the first person's teaching. Where would you be in life if you rejected that principle?

Every day there are young adults in our surrounding neighborhoods that are prevented from going to church or associating with Christians because of people who have greater influence over them. As a result, they are walking away from the church with the belief that it is too hard to be a Christian or God will never forgive them for the things they have done in their lives. As a result these evil people are taking those who are young and impressionable away from the Bible and Christianity with the hardship that it is a book of lies or it causes them to place their trust in the empty promises of an empty religion.

Imposters then confirm these influences, those who pretend to be devout Christians but make exceptions to faith in order to take people away from truth. Those who are trying to be something they are not do this. These people might think they completely understand what the Bible is teaching, but in reality, they don't have the understanding, training, or contextual knowledge to bring the Bible to life for believers today. They might pretend to have all the answers and claim to be Christians (even pastors), but they are often confused and fill in the blanks with what they think is correct or how they would like it to be.

One time my wife and I visited a church and attended a Sunday school class that was combined with all the morning classes because of a special event that was taking place later that day. The teacher was using a lesson on sin from the standard Sunday school manual. The manual read a great deal of truth, but the teacher was adding a lot to the lesson. One statement he made is, "For men not to wear a tie to church on Sunday is sinful because it doesn't present your best before God." I looked down and realized I was not wearing a tie and many of the other men were. I immediately thought of a young couple that would visit this church and hear a statement like that but didn't know there is no place in the Bible that says not wearing a tie is a sin.

Christians use verses like 2 Timothy 2:15 that says we have to present our best before God to justify their belief, but in reality, it would be completely out of context. Properly used, that verse is saying that people should present themselves as workmen who do not need to be ashamed and the great responsibility of accurately handling the word of truth. Yet imposters will take many of those verses out of context only to appear approved before man.

If we are to present ourselves as workmen who do not need to be ashamed, we don't need to wear a suit and tie to church. We should be wearing work clothes, ready to meet the needs of the congregation, shut-ins, and surrounding communities. We present our best before God emotionally, spiritually, and physically, not materially.

In the second part of 2 Timothy 3:13, Paul continues by telling Timothy that these people will become worse, deceiving and being deceived. It is an interesting contrast because the warning says evil people and imposters will become worse. This means, as they learn what works or doesn't or when they are caught in their deception, they will find new ways to deceive people into seeing things their way.

When I was younger, my dad showed us a scary movie from the early 1960s that I am sure was really scary at the time it was made, but when I saw it in the 1980s, it seemed so fake it was funny. That night we joked and laughed at the movie and had a great time making fun of it. I am sure, if that movie were remade today, it would be frightening. The tools for special effects in the 1960s were very limited compared to what we have today. Remaking any of the older movies today would increase the believability because of how people have learned to create realistic effects.

Take that same concept into the deception of others. False teachers have the ability to maintain deception based on the times. What worked to deceive people even ten years ago does not work today because of the benefit of the Internet. In the very recent past, it was almost unheard of for people to use their tablets and smartphones in worship services to read their Bibles. In the modern church age, they have the ability to quickly get on the Web and verify statements and facts that might not seem true or real to them. This allows them to challenge pastors and teachers immediately following the service once they find contradictory information.

The ease of finding information does not stop people from trying to deceive others. It only increases their need to be craftier in their deception or prey on people who do not have the ability to do their own research. Doing so empowers the deceiver while they create a following that will popularize theologies and thought processes that lead people down a path of misused statements and scriptures.

The deceiving person will lead people away from truth and direct them into error. Ministries around the world are continually combating people who would deceive others in faith and religion all the time. One particular theology that I found doing this is called "prosperity theology." This thought process asserts, the more you give to the church, the greater the blessings are. Prosperity theologians believe that, when people face trials and tribulations in life, it is because they are not paying enough homage to God. I found people who have given away their entire bank accounts for the misguided promises of an answered prayer or getting a job they desperately wanted.

In some cases, people have sold their cars and houses with the thought that they were holding on to what they currently had was too much for God to bless them with something greater. Therefore, if they sold the house they lived in and appropriately tithed the profit of the residence, God would provide them with a bigger place to live. The result of this deception is that people constantly chase a material dream, trying to replace their wants and desires above searching for a relationship with God. In other situations I have seen people pray so hard for something they wanted only to be told their prayers were not being answered because they were only tithing the minimum and they needed to give more to the church.

This type of deception draws people away from the church and into error about who God is. Because deceivers are sometimes considered trusted agents, people don't challenge them. As they are turning away from religion, they never read the verses in the Bible that talk about how God answers prayers. He will give in abundance to those who seek him, and these blessings are not limited by how much time, money, and commitment to the local church we are able to give.

Unfortunately deception within the local church is a result of being deceived. People who unknowingly deceive others usually have been deceived themselves. Paul talks about those who are being deceived in this passage as well. People who are confused by the many sacred texts that other religions are using don't invest in them because they know them to be false, but because they believe them to be true. The mistake is that many people accept the perceived truths without searching for truth themselves.

It is essential to search for truth when you hear statements that are designed to get you through struggles. More so, if you are encouraging others, it is important to know what you are saying is biblical truth. It is too easy to verify information in this day and age and not to seek and speak the truth. Where we go wrong is that we have placed so much faith in the people we believe to be experts that we do not get into our Bibles and find out the information for ourselves, even if the information does not sound right. Trying to make yourself believe something is true even when it does not sound right is the first sign that you are being deceived.

Deception means you are telling yourself something so much that you actually start believing it. There is no place in Christianity that allows for "fake it 'til you make it" theology. We have to understand in the church today that it is okay to be in desperate need of God. People don't have to walk into the church pretending like they have it all together and failing to get help because they have been deceived into thinking it is not okay to have spiritual crises or emotional issues.

As we minister to others, both inside and outside the church, it is important for us to avoid deceiving others as well as false teachers deceiving us. Combating sacred deception is extremely important to relaying God's true intention for discipleship. Paul describes this further in 2 Timothy 3:14–15. In this, he addresses prior knowledge of the Bible and what people have already learned.

The first thing Paul writes to Timothy is that he should continue in what he has already learned and firmly believed. He has the confidence of saying this because he knows what Timothy's upbringing in the Christian faith is like. When people have learned solid Bible-based gospel, they can place their confidence in what they have learned. In order to combat sacred deception, people must evaluate what is being told to them. Statements such as, "The Bible says …" without people opening the Bible can lead to greater chances of sacred deception.

When I do spiritual couples counseling, I always tell people, if you don't know where the verse is in the Bible, it is best to find it, learn it, or not use it. We should follow that simple rule because it is too easy to misuse or lead others astray. This brings a greater risk of people accusing you of being a false teacher, even when you have the best of intentions to help them.

For us to minister to others, we have to know the truth of God's Word specifically. Do this by showing others the verse and then following up with "this means …" When you do that, it gives room for conversation on the subject.

The other mistake people make in sacred deception is that they try to answer the hard questions on their own. If you don't know the answer, never be afraid to tell the person you don't know. Work with them to find someone who does know or do the research together. Too many people are embarrassed to say they don't know something in the world today. As a result, they lead others through misused and misinterpreted understandings of God's Word.

Once we have learned something and we firmly believe in what we have acquired, we have the ability to challenge those who are deceiving us, along with disciple and help people the way that God intended. The big question is: how do you know what you have learned is worth believing in? After all, there are people in the world today that firmly believe the destruction and chaos they are causing is for a worthy cause. In order to believe what is true, two things have to happen:

1. You have to do the research. People who fail to do effective self-study and believe everything people tell them is like those who adapt to lifestyle fads without having knowledge of its validity. The information at any layperson's fingertips today is too great for him or her not to have good answers for what he or she believes. However, with the abundance of information, there is also a great quantity of misinformation available. In order to do an effective self-study, you have to look at the source it is coming from. Do not take just anyone's word as the truth. People who can back what they are saying with scripture in context, along with experience and well-studied scholarship, can usually be trustworthy sources. This is not saying that people must have a PhD in order to be trustworthy. There are people without Bible degrees who have a sound understanding of the Bible.

2. Firmly believing comes from the heart. So often we have taken faith out of the equation in pursuit of knowledge. You have to believe in your heart enough to modify your lifestyle. The heart embodies everything you are made of. Historically it was believed that the heart controls the soul and mind and serves as the foundation of one's actions and passion. Once you are able to believe in something enough that your passion dictates your actions, you will see the value of spiritual living and intimate relationship with God. You will know a true teacher of faithful passion when you meet someone who not only teaches and persuades others to live a faithful lifestyle but also commits his or her own actions to the very same expectation. Many false teachers require a great deal of

their followers while holding themselves to a different standard that does not match their commands or teachings.

The other point that Paul makes in 2 Timothy is for believers to be confident in what they already know through two sources:

1. There are people who have poured their knowledge into our lives that helped us know and understand the Bible.

2. Everyone has previous and current knowledge of God's Word. Too many people downplay their knowledge of the scriptures because others intimidate them.

I had someone ask a question about dealing with cohabitation. They were told, if two people were having sex, it was okay to cohabitate because they had already become one in the eyes of God. Using Genesis 3 as the baseline for their argument, they explained that marriage was traditionally consummated by sex because it was the physical bonding of two people. Worse, they stated that God does not require paperwork for marriage. That was a governmental mandate for tax purposes.

Those who are not studied in the Bible or might be intimidated by others' knowledge of the scriptures would begin living in sin because false teachers misled them. This couple did not argue the matter because they did not know how and did not have confidence that what they already knew was enough for them to rebut the other person's misleading statements. As well, it was socially acceptable and appealed to what they wanted to hear.

In situations like this, personal confusion can unintentionally lead you down the wrong path. If you are confused in the scriptures, you can learn by taking the current knowledge of what you have read and learned and then ask questions. Comparing what you know and what other people are telling you will either help them or you learn what the truth is. If confrontation is what you are avoiding, the best thing to do is ask, "How does this relate to what the Bible says in (insert passage) …" By using this, it gives you the opportunity for exploration, clarification, and understanding so you can refute other people who have been wrongly taught or you do not wrongly teach others.

Prepare Yourself for False Teachers

While I was in military basic training, we had a section on hand-to-hand combat. This block of instruction was to teach us how to defend against attacks in close quarters combat. We worked for hours on how to block, kick, punch, and take down our aggressors. At the conclusion of training, the drill sergeant instructed us that we had just learned the basics of hand-to-hand combat. He continued to tell us that it was also just enough for us to get beat up after starting a fight. He continued with confidence that, once we get to our duty stations, leadership would teach us advanced techniques to hone our skills for hand-to-hand engagement.

As Christians, we never get that kind of warning. As new Christians, we have the basic tenets of our faith wrapped up for us in a pretty package, ready to take on the world. This knowledge is just enough to get us into heaven and a lot of trouble if we were to witness to others. Finding a good Bible teacher, having the excitement to read God's Word, asking the right questions, and listening to good lessons helps us grow spiritually. If we gain the advanced spiritual knowledge, why do we still fear questioning those who have better education, been Christians longer, or are in positions of authority?

We have to prepare ourselves for spiritual warfare, and we must be ready to recognize false teaching and clarify those who have misused the scripture for preferred theology. Paul gives us the formula for being ready in 2 Timothy 3:16–17 by instructing Timothy on what the Bible is for and how it can help us in our daily walk.

One of the most important points of instruction in this passage—and often overlooked when read is—"All Scripture is inspired by God" (2 Tim. 3:16a). Those who don't have faith in Christ challenge this statement with questions on how anyone can say that a book is God's Word when man writes it. The important aspect they miss is the word "inspired." God did not write the Bible. He *inspired* man through His Holy Spirit to write it. Because those who wrote the passages in the Bible had a deep and meaningful relationship with God, they were able to give timeless accounts and direction for people.

When you dive deeper into the passage, you learn the process necessary to use the Bible. So often people look at the second part of verse 16 as a list, not a process, but there is a method when using the Bible to encourage and instruct others. When we use the method, the Bible then becomes profitable for our growth—spiritually, emotionally, and physically.

In most cases, people do not simply benefit from a situation because they want to. In order for people to use the Bible as a profitable resource, they have to look at the benefit it provides. A process takes place in order to receive usefulness from what they hope to benefit from. If I want to benefit from a healthy lifestyle, I have to put a process in place that includes a regimen of diet and exercise. I do not lose weight, gain muscle, or become healthy simply because I want to. Rather I want to, so I go through the process to allow exercise, diet, and lifestyle to benefit my goals and me.

As Christians, we want the ability to benefit from our spiritual fitness, exercising our understanding of God's Word, ingesting what the scriptures say about being a Christian, and, most of all, living a lifestyle reflective of Christ. We have to look at the Bible as our source of spiritual direction. It prepares us to exercise our prayer relationship, and it helps us understand the importance of feeding our minds with the right things in order to be transformed by the Holy Spirit (Rom. 12:2).

If our personal lives with Christ are unhealthy, we are unable to disciple other people into healthy relationships with Christ. Not only do we have to know what the Bible says for our own personal growth, but we have to know the process for us to benefit from scriptures. Paul gives this method to Timothy when he says that all scripture is profitable for teaching, rebuking, correcting, and training in righteousness (2 Tim. 3:16b).

It is easy for people to look at this passage as a list, and at first appearances, it can be considered a list of benefits for the Bible. We have to remember that Paul's intention was not for us to choose how we would use the Bible. If that were the case, it gives way for us to pick and choose what part of the Bible we want to use to develop and disciple. If we were to look at teaching, rebuking, correcting, and training in righteousness as a process instead of a list, we become empowered and aware of viewpoints that spiritual deception corrupted.

The first step in the process of training in righteousness is to teach from the Bible. When an educator teaches his or her students, he or she uses a textbook. The textbook gives teachers a guide for what they should teach and how they should teach it. Students have at textbook that gives practical exercises along with basic instructions for how to do the work. In the same respect, a teacher of the Word should use the Bible as his or her textbook to teach from, and students should use the same scripture for learning.

When we teach people, we are using the basic principles of discipleship. Christ tells us to go and make disciples, baptizing them and teaching them as Christ has taught (Matt. 28:19). The scriptures show us how and what Christ taught his disciples. Teaching is developing these principles for growth. The teacher has an advanced knowledge of the Bible and is able to bring clarity to the student through his or her understanding. The expectation is the student eventually becomes the teacher as he or she grows in understanding God's Word.

It is also important to avoid teaching what we do not know. Too often people are afraid to say they do not know the answer to a spiritually based question. The embarrassment of not knowing the answer often results in sacred deception because the inexperienced teacher does not want the student to think he or she doesn't know the answers. It is important for people to avoid teaching what they don't know and be confident when teaching what they do know. God provided the textbook; therefore, the Bible is essential to teaching people about relationships with God, Christian living, and spiritual insight.

Once we become more experienced in God's Word, we have a better understanding how to bring up transgressions in the midst of crisis or wayward living. Rebuking an issue is difficult. So often we censure others with a focus on the person by making "you" statements followed by a definite statement similar to "always" or "need to." Instead of rebuking the person, we should concentrate on censuring the issue within Christian love. These statements sound more like, "I noticed you struggle with …" or "There are a few things that worry me with [issue]. Is everything okay?"

The biggest mistake is when we use statements like, "The Bible says you should never …" or "Don't you know [issue] is a sin according to the Bible." When we focus on the sin or the issue, we still have the ability to show love for the person. Many people make corrections with love in mind, but they discount the Holy Spirit's ability to give patience and wisdom when addressing the situation.

When we are using the scripture to rebuke someone, we are not condemning the person. Nor are we given a license to become aggressive toward an issue in order to expose him or her to everyone else. I often see Christians try to expose sin or crisis to others in an attempt to address the issues. In reality, this approach does not always get them to turn from sin, but it usually turns them away from organized religion and a community of Christians. This will take away from how God intended to support and draw them closer to Him.

Rebuking, as Paul uses in this passage, is to provide evidence of wrongdoing in order to prove with the intention of conviction. As Christians, we must avoid making emotional statements regarding a sin issue we personally despise, but we are challenged to provide scriptural proof that God despises sin and loves His people. Using the Bible to rebuke someone is the primary way we provide factual basis for God's direction with His people.

Using the Bible as a teacher and the source of proof for issues gives way to correcting. As Christians, we should not seek to destroy the person in a process of removing sin, but our goal is to restore people by removing sin. When we look at intention, we have to look at why we want to approach an issue. If the intention is to restore him or her to an upright state, we are helping the person with the right intention. If we are doing it to prove ourselves to be more righteous or better than the other person, the end result might be restoration, but the intention is for self-satisfying reasons.

The other intention is to improve life or character. Just as we restore the person spirituality, we also seek to improve his or her spiritual life and personal character. In the process of learning and having conviction in our lifestyles, we realize that the intent is not to reduce others morally, but to build up both theirs and our spiritual lifestyle. Our lives, though not made easier, are improved through our spiritual growth. Our attitudes are changed through understanding God's Word. Most of all our character is adapted because we are made a new creation (2 Cor. 5:17) through the Holy Spirit's indwelling and our eyes are opened (John 9:39) to God's plan in our lives.

This process has a goal of training in righteousness. When Paul uses the statement "trained in righteousness," he is not restarting the process but providing the summation of the process. When we train someone in righteousness, it means we have tutored him or her in the characteristics that God has intended for His creation. The culmination of teaching, rebuking, and correcting is righteousness. This concept reflects the characteristics of God through integrity, virtue, purity, correct thinking, and acting in a way that reflects God in our lives.

The development of these characteristics point toward the people we will become once we mature as Christians. For example, I was talking to a young soldier who had just been blessed with a baby boy. The statement was made that, since he had a boy to carry on his name, he did not care if he died on the battlefield. Quickly, one of the leaders said there was no way the young soldier's son could carry on his name without him being around to develop the characteristics that were associated with that name. This was a profound thought for the young soldier because he realized, without the character that only he could build in the child, the namesake was just another name.

As Christians, we have to understand that learning the characteristics of righteousness reflects the namesake of Christian. Many people simply hold the title of Christian but have no idea what characteristics are associated with that name. It is up to us to learn through biblical insight and use of the scriptures in the process of discipleship to grow and help others mature spiritually. Once this happens, we are empowered to display and teach the characteristics of Christian righteousness.

Using the above process as a list, we can pick and choose from the Holy Spirit working in the lives of people and cause them to select what they have to do to provide encouragement. God does not require his people to determine if they should teach, rebuke, correct, or train, but He does require us to disciple people. Looking at the process, we teach people about what God's Word says. Then we tell them about a sin issue, show them the right thing to do, and then train them on how to be righteous in God's eyes through the situation.

It is so easy for us to rebuke people by saying something is a sin and they should just stop. When we immediately go to rebuking someone, we are not spiritually developing people, but we are becoming judgmental and lording over them with spiritual arrogance.

I was recently teaching this study in a local church, and the consistent remark I got from those in the class was their desire to hear more about how to correct their shortcomings instead of what their failings were. They said that many people either preached against sin issues or preached about how to live for Christ; however, it is hard to hear good teaching about what is wrong and how to correct it and make sure the change is applied in everything they do.

As we look forward in the study, the outline will use the process Paul instructs Timothy with. We will learn how society misuses the statement, why the common use is generally wrong, what we should use instead to grow, and how we can help others grow in God's Word.

THE PROFIT OF SCRIPTURE

Paul answers why the process is so important in verse 17 when he gives the reason we profit from the Bible. We will first profit from being complete through spiritual growth and be equipped to refute false teachings and help other people understand the Bible. Finally, we will be able to do good works that help others see the truth of God's love.

Every Christmas, stores have a great campaign going. While it seems elementary, the signs all over toy stores and other retailers read, "Don't forget the batteries." This always serves as a reminder to consumers that, without batteries, some products are not complete and will not work as intended. I know one of the most frustrating things for me is to purchase an item with the expectation to use it, only to find out that I did not purchase the right size battery or did not have the battery to make the product work. This was evident recently when I purchased an electronic item and the remote control did not have batteries. I looked everywhere for batteries and only found sizes that did not fit.

Just like not having batteries to complete items for use, the scriptures make our Christian walk complete. It is part of our armor (Eph. 6:10–18) and the main point of defense and offense when faced with adversity. The Bible is the "sword of the Spirit" (Eph. 6:17). Can you imagine walking into a battle without your primary weapon? There is no way to address the attacks from the enemy. Yet, day in and day out, there are Christians who enter into spiritual warfare without their weapon. They believe, if they have protective gear, they will be just fine, but once Satan unleashes his demons on you, your sword of truth will allow you to defend against the evil one.

Looking at the historical aspects, even Jesus used the Bible to defend against the attacks of Satan. Of course at the time, it was not the Bible we know, but it was the written, inspired Word of God. In Matthew 4:1–11, we can see where Jesus combated Satan with the simple words, "It is written." This ability is based in the knowledge of biblical truth.

Through the Bible, we are made whole and lack nothing when we are faced with struggles and praise. Many people do not know what to say when they face others who struggle, so they often say the wrong thing. Once we know the context of the Bible and where to find words of encouragement, we are best equipped to handle every situation.

Completeness through the scripture takes away the imposed responsibility on human nature to solve the problem and serves as a crucial step in allowing God to solve the problem by speaking through His Word. A relationship with God will always give us somewhere to turn. The completeness of the Bible is not just somewhere to turn, but it is an instrument in which we are able to fill the gap of unexplained or unanswered questions regarding humankind.

When we are made complete, we have the right equipment to refute false teaching and help other people understand the Bible for themselves. If you get an incomplete toy, your children cannot play with it. Without the right batteries, you do not have the right equipment. Without the right equipment, you cannot accomplish the task.

The Bible serves as the battery, so to speak, and having the right knowledge of it will furnish you with the appropriate equipment to accomplish the ministry that God puts in your path. We have to understand, though, equipping is not a stand-alone concept. Even with the right equipment, you have to know how to use it.

I once knew someone who carried a Bible everywhere he or she went. When asked about it, he proudly said, "This is the eternal Word of God. Without it, my life would be lost." However, if asked what he used it for or how his life would be lost, he did not know what to say. Simply having a Bible is not good enough. We have to know what is in between the covers in order to use it effectively.

Once we are equipped, it is not for us to store up for personal use in case of a spiritual apocalypse, but for us to share with others. It would be easy to say that people who refuse to equip themselves with the truth are also afraid that they might have to use it to help others. On the other hand, people who fail to equip themselves might also be facing issues where they do not know how or what to use in various situations. Therefore, it is essential for those who are already equipped and know how to use the Bible to stand firm in discipleship process.

This is where Timothy gets the point. We must be complete spiritually in order to become equipped emotionally so the result is good work for the kingdom of God. This is not simply doing good deeds for people, but doing what the Holy Spirit has called you to do for others. The good works that we should do are pure of heart and diligent for the advancement of faith, not in search of self-fulfilling gratification.

I once worked with one lady who was exhausted in her ministry. After talking with her for a moment, I found that she was moving in every direction. She certainly did not depend on the Bible for direction, let alone search for the Holy Spirit's guidance. She was helping in one organization, leading another, and answering all her friend's calls for assistance, and the list goes on. She ultimately became so tired of doing good works for people that her health began to suffer. She did not understand why she was suffering so much when she felt like she was serving God. What she did not realize was that she was not serving God as much as her own internal emotional rush when she felt she had helped someone.

It is easy for us to feel great after helping someone, but if we are not doing what God has truly called us to do, we are not helping him or her the way God wants that person to find help. There are times where that individual has to go through his or her issues in order to complete and equip himself or herself and then begin doing good works for himself or herself. In most cases, the trials we face cause us to turn to God through prayer, reading the Bible, and searching for answers. We can get very tired when we try to do good works outside the Holy Spirit's intention because we are not receiving the divine power that comes with moving in the direction that God wants us to.

When we are doing good work for the kingdom, we inherently have the strength and stamina to complete that effort. The Bible will give us the answers to help us be in line with God's direction for our lives. Like many of the stories I told in this chapter, the people were subject to false teachers and misused statements that caused them to feel obligated to ministries they were never called to. And most of all, they were guided down a path that leads to exhaustion that takes you from experiencing God's intention for great joy.

Breaking down these three concepts, one can see the power that the scripture holds for God's people. When we use it in the right context and the way God intended, we no longer simply profit from the Bible but gain a way of life. The new birth that takes place will change how we view the social and societal norms that say the Bible is just a book or we have the right to manipulate it for our personal needs. Instead we are empowered to use the scriptures in a way that grows God's people, brings sight to those who don't know God, and serves as our proof that God was, is, and will always be active in everyone's lives throughout all time.

As we understand the scripture at a deeper level, we have to be confident to refute false teaching. Most of all, this deeper knowledge will help us recognize what false teaching is. Spiritual deception only gets worse as people place their trust in their own understanding and not God's (Prov. 3:5). It is easy for us to think that church people tell others to read the Bible because they think that is just what they are supposed to do. But looking at the passage from 2 Timothy, you can see where the Bible serves a much greater purpose in our Christian walk.

It holds profit for us that we might go through a process of preparation in order to be complete for each task that God puts in our path. These tasks are not mandatory for us to get into heaven, but they are essential for us to show God's light in us to others in the midst of darkness. As we progress in the lessons, allow the light of the Holy Spirit to shine brighter in you, clarifying the Word and completing you for all good works.

Self-Reflection or Small Group Discussion Questions

1. What experiences have you had while ministering to people of other faiths, and were you able to refute their claims of faith?

2. Have you ever encountered a false teacher? When did you realize he or she was not teaching the truth?

3. Have you ever walked away from positive influences because someone else convinced you otherwise?

4. How do false teachers affect your faith?

5. What was the most impactful teaching you have ever received from someone in your life?

6. Is there someone who provided discipleship in your life? What things did he or she do to help you mature spiritually?

7. Do you have a tendency to use the scriptures as a process or list, as 2 Timothy 3:16 describes?

8. How has the Bible completed, equipped, and helped you do good work for the kingdom?

9. How have you gotten off track doing good work to feel good about yourself but think you are doing everything with God's direction?

10. How can you realign yourself with God's direction for your life?

---------- C H A P T E R 1 ----------

SESSION 2: OVERWHELMED

Sometimes when we get overwhelmed, we forget how big God is.

—author unknown

"God will never give us more than we can handle, right, Chaplain? I mean that's what the Bible says, right?" This is a statement I hear constantly, and it makes me cringe with the thought that our expectation of God is to give us light burdens. The issue with this expectation is that heavy burdens come our way almost constantly. This is a natural part of life. What is heavy for one person might be easy for another.

Throughout my ministry, I have heard a lot of people talk about how overwhelmed they are in their circumstances. While working in the hospital environment, I saw parents who faced some of the most difficult events in their lives. As a military chaplain, I see families who have faced death, divorce, illness, and all the other issues that come with living life.

In addition, this statement expresses the thought that God gives us everything we face, good or bad. This is also disastrous because we don't realize that God does not give us everything. Rather He allows some things to happen. We will get into that later. However, we face long journeys in life thinking that, no matter how stressful or full of emotional difficulties our paths are, we should not and cannot get drained because "God doesn't give us more than we can handle."

Eventually everyone reaches his or her limit, and that is why so many people who face stress in life believe that God is dysfunctional in some way. They have received more than they can handle. They are ready to give up

1

on their situations, their faith, and, in some cases, their lives. Why? Because someone told them that God would never give them more than they could handle, and in the midst of this, they are at the point of having more than they can handle. It seems as if God is trying to kill them more than He is loving and caring for them. We get overwhelmed and remain convinced that God protects His people by keeping them from experiencing the trials and events in their lives that might be too heavy to bear.

While we will look at why bad things happen to God's people later, we will concentrate here on the fact that people hear this statement day in and day out. Yet they still feel overwhelmed by life's circumstances. We become discouraged by circumstances, and it becomes easy for us to ask the question: Where is God if He will never give me more than I can handle?

This statement was the most misused words of encouragement that I heard from pastors and other ministry leaders in the hospital environment. It seemed as if people who did not know what to say for encouragement would just say that God would not give them more than they could handle. Nevertheless, the fact is that God does give us more than we can handle. It remains that, when we are overwhelmed and stressed, God has not left our sides. Even more, there is no way we can change the fact that nowhere in the Bible does it say God will never give us more than we can handle.

The culture today uses this statement to provide encouragement to others because they feel this statement will cause us to believe God always protects us. People mumble the same words to themselves with the thought that if they say them enough, they will be true. On top of that, we can recognize many who say them to provide their own encouragement that things can get worse and God will provide the strength they need to get through a situation.

When I look at how this phrase is used to encourage others with emotional issues, I can see how we run into situations where people are hopeless and cannot see how God is involved in their lives every day. No wonder the suicide rate in the world is so high. If I were facing emotional problems that created symptoms leading to depression, hopelessness, anxiety, or traumatic stress disorders, hearing that God will never give me more than I can handle might not provide the encouragement I was looking for. This discounts the validity or seriousness associated with emotional strife.

Those who are facing these issues become overwhelmed because of a Christian culture that believes everything emotionally deficient comes from sin. When this happens, people who are suffering emotionally doubt their true emotional situations because they believe God would never give them anything they could not handle. As a result, they progress deeper into their emotional strife, and it becomes so overwhelming that they feel as if there is no place to turn. At that point, turning to God even becomes hopeless.

Hopelessness is not confined to emotional strife either. Once again, when we face physical ailments, the emotional aspect is brought into the picture, but sometimes we need to be encouraged physically. We use this statement when addressing physical issues because we do not know what else to say. Unless you have medical training or completely understand everything the doctor has said to you about a personal ailment, "take two aspirin and call me in the morning" is not a very good response.

We know that, when we visit our friends in the hospital or we are sick ourselves, we do not have the training or authority to recommend treatment plans. When physical ailments discourage us, the idea that God never gives us more than we can handle has the ability to give us comfort, but theologically it just is not true. In many cases, it becomes empty encouragement. For the person who has cancer, it certainly seems like more than he or she can handle. Despite the physical stressors, we continually try to encourage people with this thought. However, if you are experiencing a physical overload, it's easier to become consumed by the thought that God has left you in the wake of Satan's destruction.

Between God's hand of protection and Satan's destruction, we can develop an understanding of true spiritual warfare. We have to understand that people do become spiritually discouraged. Some of you reading this book right now might be feeling that way. Spiritually, you might feel like God has left your side. When someone does not know what to say as he or she comes alongside you for support, it is easy for us to go deeper in spiritual despair. When we talk about God never giving us more than we can handle, it is easy to believe that God is not giving us anything at all.

The silence of God is often more than we can handle when we have a close relationship with Him.

In the midst of spiritual discouragement, we find out that God has not left us, but we have failed to see where God is involved in our lives. Most often, it is because we are facing physical or emotional turmoil that has caused us to look for answers. Despite the spiritual encouragement that God will never give us more than we can handle, we still feel overwhelmed. Such a succinct statement then begins to sound like a standard go-to response instead of genuine encouragement.

False teachers will convince others of two things when this statement is made:

1. They make people believe the statement is true. The issue with this is that God does give us more than we can handle and oftentimes much more than we can handle. He does not give us more than He can handle though. If we never experienced more than we could handle, we would never be able to overcome issues through God's power. We would always face life with ease, and we would ultimately believe we have no need for God in our lives. The challenges in our lives prepare us to walk alongside others as they face similar challenges, which in turn better equips us for God's ministry.

2. False teachers convince themselves that these are the words of Paul in the Bible. They search repeatedly in the Bible, but they do not seem to find the verse anywhere. Because it is what has always been said to them by others in the church, they believe it has to be in the Bible. We wrongly ascribe many statements and verses to the Bible because we have always heard these statement simply repeated by others.

This statement is said and attributed to the Bible via lack of knowledge, or it is attributed to the Bible by those who have twisted the verse most commonly associated with it. Looking at how people modify the verse, we can see how our society has misused it as a feel-good scripture in life's struggle as opposed to how it was intended to be used for the first-century church.

While "God will never give you more than you can handle" seems like a biblical statement, looking at the verse it is associated with reveals a completely different meaning. The verse that is most closely associated with this statement is 1 Corinthians 10:13. If you look at the verse, you can see that it does not even come close to addressing lives that are difficult and overwhelming. Instead Paul is talking to the church about temptations.

Looking at the Context

An older gentleman went to the doctor for some issues with joint pain. After a full workup of tests and a complete examination, the doctor came in and told him, "I have some good news and some bad news. Which do you want first?" Being a cancer survivor, it was difficult for the older gentleman to hear the bad news. Immediately his thoughts began to race. *Is the cancer back? Is there something worse going on with me?* With a desire to ease his thoughts, the elderly gentleman asked for the bad news.

The doctor said in very jovial voice, "You are getting old!"

A sigh of relief exited the gentleman, as he already knew that. If that were the bad news, the good news had to be great. Simply put, all the issues he went to see the doctor with was normal for a man of his age. He then followed up with a simple warning. He had to stop running so much because it was destroying his knee joints and lower back.

In context, this is pretty funny doctor humor, but out of context, it can seem cruel and disheartening. But we are not much different when we take verses from the Bible to fit our needs. Funny jokes can soften the blow, just like misused statements can soften the hurt and pain one might be feeling, but out of context, we find that the hurt and pain can be worse as we also feel betrayed by those who so animatedly encouraged us with their misused words.

In order to understand the one verse associated with this statement, we have to look at the entire passage in context for the event. Looking at 1 Corinthians 10:1–21, we can see the good news, the bad news, and the warning that Paul gives for his people. Considering these three aspects, we are able to clearly see that God is focused on temptations, not distress. Moreover, Paul is giving encouragement to those who are being tempted and relaying a message of the importance of unity through Christ.

THE BAD NEWS

The bad news in this passage is that we serve a jealous God and, at one point, a vengeful God (Deut. 6:14–15). People do not like to hear that. They like the all-loving God that cradles the world in His arms. However, when Paul is talking about this to the first-century church, he is reminding them about the God of the Old Testament. He writes to them about the God who required atonement that demanded obedience.

In the midst of that though, we have to understand that God also understood we, as a creation, were sinners and could not achieve the level of obedience He required. Therefore, He became that atonement for us through His Son, Jesus Christ. This was not so we could have the freedom to sin without consequence, but so we could repair our ability to have a relationship with Him. It is important for us to understand that God does not strike us down as He did to those in the Old Testament for disobedience, but one day we will see his vengeance as we stand before judgment.

I believe we will have to answer to a few things when we do stand before judgment, but one of them is foundational to our relationship with God. Paul relays this aspect in verse 7 when he mentions idolaters. Just as the issues were prevalent to those in the first-century church, the bad news for us today is that we are idolaters too. Many people forget that anything taking away from relationship with God becomes idolatrous behavior.

In a hectic life that seems to be moving at the speed of sound sometimes, we lose our time with God. This concept is easy to remember because we always say to make time for God. Time is so valuable to us. We fill our schedules and take pride in telling people how busy we are. When I counsel people on time management, maybe one in five schedules I look at has time for God in it.

It is interesting, if you were to ask people if they could have anything in the world, they would not say a less hectic life, but more hours in the day so they could complete the tasks they have. We as a society make time to work out and visit friends, and we even overtask ourselves vocationally, yet we do not have time to develop our relationship with God.

Lacking the ability to develop our relationship with God only leads to sin issues that cause us to turn our back on Him. Once we turn our back on God, we are committing idolatry just the same. Simply by consciously engaging in sinful behavior, we are making a choice. We decided at some point that the sin issue was more important to us at that moment than pleasing God. Thus, it takes away from our relationship with God and causes us to search for forgiveness in an effort to repair that relationship.

Using instances of God's wrath for the people in the Old Testament, Paul begins to relate examples of what happened when they did not have the forgiveness of the cross. Looking at these lessons, people in the Old Testament faced the same issues Paul warns about in the New Testament, and still today we are suffering through the idolatrous issues of adultery (verse 8), testing Christ (verse 9), and complaining about God's blessings in our lives (verse 10).

I always say to remember that adultery with an "a" will lead every Christian into idolatry with an "i." The concept is simple. While Paul was referring to adultery as the sexual act with anyone other than one's spouse, today the concept of adultery is much different.

Just as idolatry is allowing anything in life to replace your relationship with God, adultery is allowing anything in life to replace your relationship with your spouse. When couples come to me for counseling and I ask, "Are you having an affair?" they are quick to respond with, "No, I am not sleeping with anyone." After we investigate the issue, they are correct. They are not sleeping with anyone. The unfortunate part is that they are so in love with other things that their marriages are suffering.

In younger couples that get married, sometimes the men are so involved in the latest video game that they lose sight of their responsibilities to the family. Some people do not feel comfortable talking to their spouse about issues because it might lead to argument, so they find another person to confide in. Others do not feel like they have a spiritual partner they can connect to God with, so they go to church and find another person with whom they can grow spiritually.

Knowingly and unknowingly, they engage in the spiritual, emotional, and physical feel-good scenario that slowly tears them away from God. Going to church becomes more about seeing the other person than it does about growing spiritually. Spending time in conversation becomes more about emotional fulfillment than it does about social interaction. Finally, physical interaction becomes lustful desire more than an ordained event reserved for marriage.

Once we enter into adultery, we are testing the limits of forgiveness and grace. When I ask couples why is it easier to argue with their spouse than their work mates, the answer is always the same. They reply because their spouse is not going anywhere. Unfortunately, too many couples have tested the limits of their spouse's forgiveness and grace, and the result is divorce.

We have the same confidence when we enter into a relationship with God. We continue to sin because we know God is not going anywhere. It is easy for us to feel like we are covered and God will always forgive us; therefore, we do not have to grow spiritually. As a result, we test Christ in many aspects of our lives. Testing and verifying is a natural reaction when something seems too good to be true or we are not sure of the call.

I am guilty of testing God in some aspects. When I graduated from high school, I attended a local Bible college in Ohio. While there studying secondary education, I felt a call to ministry. Not wanting to go into the field, I ran from the call for nearly seven years. I dropped out of school and joined the army. When I was in my late twenties, I received the call again, but this time I felt I had done too much in my life to be worthy of a call to ministry.

At a stronger level, God began to speak to me through other people. Soon I gave in. I expressed to God that if I were truly called to ministry, I would go into seminary, but I would take one semester, and if I were successful, I would continue. I applied and was accepted. I attended my first semester, but just to be sure, I took two classes. For those of you who know, introduction to Greek and introduction to Hebrew should never be taken in the same semester, but I did that. I wanted to be certain that God was calling me to ministry, and I was going to make it as difficult as possible. At the end of the semester, I received my grades, the determining factor for my career in ministry. The results, as you might wonder, were an A in Hebrew and a B in Greek.

We have to learn the fine line between testing God and verifying His direction. When we test Him, we will generally be put in our place. When we verify, God will provide the confirmation needed in His way. In this passage, Paul is talking about those who test God in order to see if His wrath or blessings will come true. Testing is something that brings doubt in our relationship with God. If we are not tempted to test God, it is because we are confident in the direction God is leading. On the contrary, if we are tempted to test God, it is because we lack the faith to trust Him.

The final form of idolatry Paul brings to light is complaining about God's blessings. Throughout the Bible, people complain about what they do not have and want more than they praise for what they do have and need. Today we see people complain about what they do not have and want more than they praise for what they do have and need.

We are always striving for the next rung in the ladder, we are always in a hurry to get to the next red light, and we are always dissatisfied with what God has given us because the people next door seem like they have so much more. We are on a quest to get the next qualification because that is what the other person has. My wife and children have wanted a fire pit in the backyard for years. While this sounds like a good idea, all I can see sometimes is two preteens running around the yard with flaming sticks in their hands, so I resisted it. Not to mention we could not afford what it would take to make one correctly. My wife, who prayed it up, found an ad for free red brick on a local website. As we were driving out of the neighborhood where we got the brick, we began to talk about what the people who lived in the houses did to afford such expensive living arrangements.

We were not comparing ourselves to them, but for every person in that neighborhood, I am sure there was a person in their workplace wanting to be like them. The desire to have what everyone else has results in debt. I am not just talking about monetary debt, but spiritual, emotional, and physical voids that will never be paid off. Just when people get to where they think they will be comfortable, they find someone or something else they want to chase after.

Finding joy in God's blessing goes far beyond "what's in it for me," but it extends to how God has given to us so we can grow and be healthy— spiritually, emotionally, and physically. It is impossible to chase after God if we are chasing after everything but Him.

These three things take us away from relationship with God, but they are not the only things that we face in the world today. So often people think, because they pray or go to church on Sunday morning, their spiritual lives are completely intact. In order to evaluate the idolatrous behaviors in your life, you can use a simple exercise. By using a simple scaling technique, you can rate your relationship with God on a scale from one to ten. By selecting one, you are saying you have a very limited relationship with God, and a ten is the best it could possibly be here on earth.

Once you have selected the number that honestly describes your relationship with God, draw a horizontal line on a piece of paper. Above the line, draw an arrow pointing up, and below the line, draw an arrow pointing down. Next to the arrow pointing up, write all the things in your life that brings the number higher than one. Beside the arrow pointing down, write all the things in your life that bring the number lower than a ten. Once you have done this, you will see all the things that take away from your relationship with God. If you are honest with yourself in this exercise, you will be able to develop a game plan to improve your relationship with Him.

Improving our relationship with God should be one of the primary goals for our lives. Not everyone cares about having a strong relationship with God, but many people only want Him as a "hip pocket" resource in case of emergencies. We have to remember, if God's number-one desire is to have relationship with His creation, than Satan's number-one desire is to destroy that association. How does he do it? Through tempting you with pleasures that draw you away from time with God.

The Good News

I love good news, especially on a bad day where I need to hear something positive. The one thing that bothers me, though, is when the good news starts like bad news. This is what Paul does when he relays the good news in verse 13. He eases into the good news with the notion that everyone faces temptation, but then he progresses to how faithful God is.

We have to remember that we look at this verse when we get the statement that God will never give us any more than we can handle. The first twelve verses of this chapter have focused on temptation and idolatry in three specific areas, and now we come to the hard truth. Everyone is tempted. We are tempted to walk away from God. We are tempted through sinful eyes, lustful hearts, anger, deceit, power, fame, and glory. Society has provided us a number of ways to be tempted every day.

Paul is specific in telling the church, "No temptation has overtaken you except what is common to humanity" (verse 13a). This being the case, we understand the parameters of temptations. The temptations never change, but the methods will depend on what we expose ourselves to.

There are many parts of sexual immorality, and temptation can come through the computer, television, and various other means. All who engage in these immoral acts are tempted through sexual addictions but fulfill them through differing means.

Simply put, temptation overtakes all of humanity. That means Satan is not partial to any particular person, and God is not biased to extend grace to any particular person. It also means that you are not alone. You are not standing in a desert waiting for an oasis, hoping that someone like you will come along to provide some level of normalcy to your idolatrous temptations.

This also means that, with every temptation you face, you run the high risk of falling to it. Satan knows when, where, and how to tempt us. Society knows how to provide its execution. If we are in the flesh, we have to remember that temptation does not escape anyone. Even Jesus was tempted (Matt. 4:1–11). The difference is that His was met with divine resistance.

The good news continues because God is faithful. It's a simple word that describes God's interaction with humanity, but many people lose sight of what it actually means to be "faithful." When we say that God is faithful, we are saying that He is true to His Word. God is worthy of our trust in what He says He will do. When someone is faithful, he or she is trustworthy. When God says He will never leave or forsake you (Deut. 31:6), it means He will go with you through the best and worst parts of your life.

Paul is not just talking about how faithful God is by sticking to our sides, but also how faithful He is when we depend on Him in times of trouble. When we depend on God, He is faithful enough to prevent temptation that will completely overtake you. Looking at this verse, the word that stands out is "allow." This means that God is always providing oversight to our temptations. We are only tempted to the extent that God allows.

We have to understand this key point. There is a big difference between God allowing temptation and tempting us Himself. God will never tempt his people into sin issues. This would be like a friend tantalizing you into stealing from him or her. It just would not make sense because temptation can lead to destruction of the relationship that people have with one another. Therefore, God does not seek to destroy His relationship with you, but draw you closer.

God desires a closer relationship with His creation; therefore, He positions us to become closer despite the temptations. He allows it so we can become stronger in our faith. This is a faith that says, "Without God, there is no way I can have the power to overcome this issue. Without God, I would submit to every temptation that comes my way." We have to remember, though, Satan is the tempter, and he knows exactly what you will fall to every time it is put in front of you. God allows it because our faith that He will give us strength to get through it grows within the ability to resist temptation. The desire to be closer in relationship with His creation is exactly how God positions us.

It is not an evil plot to get people to run back to Him. It is the relationship of a Father with a growing child. You have to let them fall before you come and save them. Just like every bad decision I made in my life, my father allowed it to happen so I would learn through life's experiences. Just as my father remained available to me, God is always there to help pick me up when I fall.

Paul says there is always a way out of temptation. For this, we understand that God is the way out. Just as He allows it, He can also stop it from happening. People do not realize that God will always provide a way out when we depend on Him. Looking at this verse along with the previous twelve, we see the importance of overcoming temptations, not the fact that God will never give you more than you can handle. In fact, it might be the opposite. God will allow you to receive temptation, not trials, in life. The important fact is that He does not tempt you beyond the ability for us to run back to Him for help.

As we look at the good news, God will never allow the temptation to completely block our sight of Him. When we are tempted, God draws the line at anything that will block His ability to rescue us from total submersion in sin. It is possible, though, for us to become overtaken by sin and temptations to the point where we fail to see God. Just as we can run toward God, we also have the ability to run from Him.

Make no mistake. People run from God and toward temptation every day. Our world is consumed by it, and so people lose sight of who God is through the blind abandon of sin. As a result, Paul must give the warning and understanding of God's people.

The Warning

When I was younger, my father would give me advice on certain matters. Often I would roll my eyes and keep moving in the direction I wanted to. Eventually my actions of turning from my father's advice led to living a life running from God. The rest of my story is the thing that got me back in the church was something my mother told me after my father passed away. She said my dad always wondered why I turned out the way I did. He said he raised my sister and me in the church the same way. He did devotions with us and mentored us in the Christian faith. However, I ran from it, and she married a pastor.

This changed my life forever, but the issue I face every day is the desire to have my father's council in ministry and the scripture. I was prideful and thought I did not need God or advice about Him. Now I know I needed that, but I had to fall before I realized how important it truly was.

People say the quickest way to fall down a mountain is to stand at the top with confidence. Paul makes this clear in verse 12 as he is specific that if you overcome, be careful or you might fall. Temptations are not overcome permanently. They are overcome one at a time, instance by instance, and, most of all, hour by hour. You might not have the desire or temptation for something because of your faithful Christian walk, but just as Jesus was in the desert, tired, hungry, and thirsty, Satan appears.

Satan waits for opportunity to destroy. He attacks when you least suspect it, especially when you think you have overcome it. I knew someone who used to smoke. He quit almost twenty years ago, but every time he walks through a cloud of smoke, he takes a deep breath. He says he does not smoke anymore, but he still loves the smell. Toying with temptation like that keeps the door cracked for you to fall. Alcoholics should not go to the bar for a cola because they will be tempted to add whiskey to their drink. We have to remember that overcoming one instance is not overcoming the hidden nature of your temptations. We have to run as far away as possible from the things that take us from God so we can avoid falling after we have overcome.

When I was in the first grade, I allowed a classmate to convince me that cheating on a spelling test would help me get a good grade. With a plan in mind, I prepared the paper so I would be able to look at it during the test.

Unfortunately I put the paper on my desk upside down and backward. Regardless of the fact that I could not cheat because I was unable to see the words, the teacher saw me looking and gave me an automatic zero on the test. I went to the principal's office, and my parents were called.

My walk home from school that day was the longest I think I ever had the entire time I attended grade school. I was so afraid to stand in front of my father and tell him what had happened. The fact that I had disappointed and most likely embarrassed him in the small town was horrible. No matter, I had to face the truth. I attempted to cheat, I was caught, and I had to face the consequences.

Sometimes we are like that with God. We fall to temptation, realize what we have done wrong, and fear disappointing God. As a child, I had to go home despite the discipline and grace that would await me. Humanity tends to do the opposite. Those who fully understand the grace of God will always run to Him when they fall or fail. There are those that do not run to God. Instead they feel as though God could never forgive them for what they have done, and so they continue in their sin. While avoiding the prospect of spiritual conviction, people enter a series of misfortune that takes them deeper in their sin issues.

Human nature will always drive people down a path that can lead to sin or righteousness. Unfortunately when temptations present themselves, most people will give into sin. This is why Paul writes that we should flee from idolatry in verse 14. Our ability to flee from the things that take away from our relationship with God empowers us to face Him with the confidence that grace abounds when we do fall to temptation.

Fleeing from idolatry is the practice of turning away from sin and temptation and turning toward the blessings of God. In the midst of turmoil, those blessings are immediately grace, peace, and God's mercy. When we humbly approach God with our trials and suffering, there is no question these blessings will be extended. Having that confidence is the beginning of the healing process when the result of our sin turns to pain and suffering—spiritually, emotionally, and physically.

The healing process is important because there is a connection among all people through the communion table. The understanding we can see here is that Christ serves as the common bond among those who have believed in their hearts and confessed with their mouths that Jesus is Lord. Paul gains his realization of this concept on the road to Damascus when Christ appears to him and says, "I am Jesus, the one you are persecuting" (Acts 9:5).

What Christ is saying through this passage is that He dwells in all people, and by dwelling in all people, when they are hurting, He is hurting. And when He is hurting, the body is hurting. We are interconnected through the blood and body of Christ. That connection serves as a warning against idolatry because, once we allow idolatry to enter into our lives, it eventually affects the church.

Idolatry, as seemingly harmless as it can feel, draws us away from using our gifts of the Holy Spirit as God intended for the church. Each of us has an opportunity to serve the church in a way that helps us grow in spirituality as well as righteousness. We have to heed this warning because we cannot continue to be Christians involved in idolatrous relationships and expect it will not affect the church in some way or another.

Regardless if you are in a mega or small church, you cannot escape how God deals with your heart. When we enter idolatrous relationships, God will deal with your heart in a way that reflects the attitude in which you attend church. We have to ask ourselves why we even go to church. If it is because attending church is what you have always done or you are just going so your kids get a solid moral background, you might be sitting in the pew for the wrong reasons. The attitude of being in church is not only to grow your own relationship with God but so others might benefit from you exercising your gifts.

I see this the most on Wednesday nights at some of the local churches. Parents either hang out in the parking lot talking with their friends or do the classic drive-by drop-off. While they see it as free time to relax with friends or run errands, the children are learning about a God with whom their parents just do not have time to have a relationship with. We become more excited about filling our thoughts and minds with the latest parent gossip or catching up on the latest and greatest television show.

We spend time feeding our minds and hearts with temporary pleasures that will eventually go to the wayside, and ultimately we will be faced with eternal judgment. For this reason, Paul presses the point at the end of the passage that we cannot eat at the table of God and demons. We have to choose one or the other. The attitudes in which you approach others reflect how you are nourishing your heart.

I absolutely love pizza, a good, hot, steaming pie with the little pepperonis that get crispy on the edge as they curl up. I throw some pineapple on it, and I have my favorite Friday night meal. If I am able, I could eat an entire large pie in one sitting. I have an issue though. First, that would be gluttony, and second, I have a responsibility to stay fit. Something happened to me when I left my twenties. I think they call it getting older, but all I know is that I can't eat anything I want without having to run ten miles to lose all the calories.

I cannot expect to eat all the junk food I want and still be healthy at the same time. In the same respect, Christians cannot expect to entertain sin issues that take them away from God and have a strong and solid relationship with Him at the same time. Just as there are consequences for my actions if I eat unhealthy, like heart disease, high blood pressure, cholesterol, or severe obesity, there are costs for living a life devoid of a relationship with God.

I will not know I am about to have a heart attack from poor eating habits until I have a heart attack. There are warning signs, but my mentality would be to just push through or think it is something else. In the same respect, there are warning signs to poor spiritual health, but oftentimes we don't think it is affecting our spiritual well-being until after it is too late.

It is easy for people to get away with sin issues. After falling into temptation, they believe their habit is not hurting anything. If no one knows what he or she is dealing with, how can it hurt the body of Christ? Simply put, it puts a barrier up between Christ and your heart that can be penetrated, but with every act of idolatry, that barrier becomes thicker and thicker.

When most people leave the church completely, it is because they have slowly placed distance between God and them. They might make excuses that the pastor isn't preaching the way they like, the people don't really care about them the way they want, or the programs they are looking for are not offered at that church. They make excuses about their prayer lives as well, for example, they do not have time, the kids prevent them from getting close to God, or they work too hard to be burdened with trying to do devotions. We have to understand that we never make excuses for the things we want to do, and when temptations overcome us, we begin to pull away from church because we just do not want to be convicted.

In the passage above, we can see where God will not allow us to be tempted beyond what we can handle, but in many cases, He will always give us more than we can handle. The verse focuses on the temptations of sin and idolatry. Facing these temptations pulls us away from God and deteriorates the connection we can have with the Holy Spirit. We can have confidence that God will also provide a way out of the temptation. Often this escape is through a relationship with God. Our ability to run from temptation into the arms of an all-loving Father empowers us to avoid idolatrous behaviors but usually does not prevent us from engaging in them.

WHAT SHOULD WE USE INSTEAD

Avoiding idolatrous behaviors at all costs is a wonderful start to Christian living, but what about the original issues we face with being overwhelmed?

1. If we are going to encourage people with the statement that God would never give them more than they can handle, we must have the confidence that pain and suffering doesn't come from God, so there is no way He can or will give us more than we can handle. He does allow us to be tempted, which can result in pain and suffering. It is every Christian's responsibility to provide encouragement through a statement that is first in the Bible and, second, focuses more on circumstances. This will help people engage in the Bible at a greater level.

2. We are creatures of comfort, which, good or bad, loves company. Think about it. When we are in the hospital, it gives us comfort to have someone sit with us even if all we do is sleep. When we are sick at home, we love to be around people or know they are there. There is no difference when we face trials in life. Not only do we want someone by our sides, but also we want people who have experienced the same trials in life. We hope they would be able to relate to our situation a little bit better. If we know someone has overcome similar experiences as us, we are more apt to heed his or her warning.

When we look at 2 Corinthians 1:3–10 or James 1:2–4, it is easy to see that Paul and James are struggling with how God plays a role in their situations. What is not apparent is how God plays a role in our circumstances through these verses. Breaking both of them down, we are able to relate to their experiences much easier and understand that facing adversity is a universal and timeless life event.

2 Corinthians 1:3–10

This passage shows the emotional and physical turmoil that can take place in the midst of hopelessness, even to the point of death. Beyond that, it gives the encouragement of hope through Christ's saving power.

Suicide is an epidemic that has plagued our society today. Some would say that this is because we as a society have created an environment of loopholes. If we are not happy with something or we want out of a contract, we simply look for the loophole. If we want out of our marriage, we can file for divorce, and the list goes forever. However, this "loophole" mentality opens the door to thoughts that if life is too difficult, we can get out of it by taking our own lives.

I know that is a bold statement that can create a great deal of controversy for many people. Let me be clear though. I am not discounting the emotional involvement of hopelessness, depression, anxiety, and all the other reasons associated with those who contemplate suicide. The point I am making is that suicide is the result of hopelessness caused by being overwhelmed with life's situations. The thousands of people I have talked with who were contemplating suicide have the same apprehension. They are facing overwhelming trials that have blocked their ability to see beyond the circumstances and have the future hope of perseverance to overcome the situation.

This is also not discounting the thousands of people who have overcome suicidal ideations and all the others who have never looked at suicide as an option to overcome their circumstances. If we look at 2 Corinthians 1:3–10, we can begin to pick out the overwhelming life circumstances that Paul reveals to the church of Corinth.

When we are overwhelmed, we look for comfort. In the passage relating to temptations above (1 Cor. 10:16–17), we see where Paul instructs the church that we are connected through the communion table (the cup and bread), and through that, the Holy Spirit interconnects us all. Paul brings this understanding to light in 2 Corinthians 1:3–7 by relaying God as the comforter. In verse 4 he writes, "He comforts us in all our affliction, so that we may be able to comfort those who are in any kind of affliction, through the comfort we ourselves receive from God."

In all things, we can find the peace of God through God Himself. More importantly, He comforts in our entire affliction. This means there is nothing we will experience that God will not provide peace, as long as we take the time to yield to our circumstances and allow the Holy Spirit to provide for our emotional strife. This sounds easy in many cases, but in reality when you are facing overwhelming circumstances in life, our natural response is to be defensive or offensive in the situation. If that is the case, we take control over our circumstances.

We can learn another thing from this verse; we have a responsibility to others as well. Paul mentions this twice in the first part of this passage (v. 3–7). The first time we can see this is in verse 4 when Paul writes, "So that we may be able to comfort those who are in any kind of affliction." The second time we see this responsibility is not as apparent but still important. He writes in verse 7, "Because we know that as you share in the sufferings, so you will share in the comfort."

The lesson we can take away from this is that we have a responsibility to help comfort those who are hurting because we too have received God's comfort. More than that, we are able to share in the comfort because we are connected through the blood and body of Christ.

Instead of telling people that God will never give you more than you can handle, we can tell others that they will receive comfort from God by connecting to a community of believers that will not only share in their hardship but share in the comfort as well.

Have you ever been in a situation where you hurt for someone else? Things may weigh heavy on your mind because you know someone who is hurting and overwhelmed. When I hurt for other people, I know I am sharing in their affliction, but sometimes I cannot do anything to help them.

When we share in the affliction, sometimes someone else's circumstances consume us. When this happens, his or her crisis soon becomes ours, and eventually no one will be comforted in the situation. When I was going through my crisis and trauma training, one of the first things we were taught was not to match your emotion with the other person's crisis. Despite what we see or experience, it is important for us to maintain the calming presence in any situation. When we try to help other people, we should use the same principle of comfort.

People are coming to you for help because they respect the fact that you might be able to assist them through their crisis. Their expectation is that you can have an objective point of view that will bring comfort to the situation because they can't see their way past the crisis. You can only share in that level of comfort with others when you are able to allow the Holy Spirit to do His work.

Many of us can relate to being overwhelmed. Some of you reading this book right now are probably overwhelmed by life's circumstances, and Paul was no different. In verse 8, he brings to light the personal struggles and hopelessness in his own life and ministry. He identifies two emotions in this passage. First, he writes, "We were completely overwhelmed—beyond our strength." This is a feeling of stress. Have you ever been so overwhelmed that you did not know how to endure the next thing that life would bring your way? Paul did in Asia, and he is sharing that level of stress with the church in Corinth because he knows that we as believers "share in the sufferings … [and] share in the comfort" (v. 7b).

The second is the feeling of hopelessness. Paul specifically writes, "We were even despaired of life. Indeed, we personally had a death sentence within ourselves" (v. 8b–9a). Those who have ever had suicidal thoughts can relate to this feeling. The fact is that you are so overwhelmed and hopeless that you were despaired of life and given yourself a death sentence as the only logical means of escape. The feeling that you want to die is scary, but Paul writes that it was not to take their own lives but to trust in God who raises the dead (v. 9b).

Within this statement, we can begin to understand the importance of hope. Paul is talking about emotional, not literal, death. It is the feeling that nothing matters, and you are not able to feel emotion. Happiness, sadness, excitement, and even pleasure are feelings that have gone to the wayside, and the only thing you feel is emptiness. It is important to understand this. God, through the comfort of His people, is able to bring you back from that despair of death.

Through God, we can have the confidence that He had, will, and will always deliver us (v. 10). This is a past, present, and future statement. We have confidence that God will bring us through whatever situation we are facing right now because He has brought us through situations in the past. We can also face tomorrow because God "will deliver us again."

We have to understand this. God does not select which of our battles He will help us conquer. His intention is to bring us through every battle we face. We fail in this confidence because our human nature tends to select the battles that we bring to God. When this happens, we just have the expectation that God is supposed to bring us through our battles, and if He doesn't, we get upset, as if He lets us down because we didn't go to Him in the first place.

When I am running, one of the routes I take has a long stretch on it that lasts about three-quarters of a mile. When I get halfway through that stretch, I look forward and think about how much further I have to travel to get past it, and on the hard days, it seems like forever. In many cases, I have to just put my head down and take it one step at a time. Before I know it, I am rounding the corner and heading on to new scenery. Sometimes I have to look back and see how far I have traveled in order to have the confidence to move forward. After all, the quickest way through something is not to go back, but to push forward.

When we look at our situation and how God plays a role in it, we have to examine it in the same way. When life is getting so overwhelming that we are having a hard time seeing the finish line, we look back and see where God has brought us through all the other overwhelming times in our lives. This gives us confidence because we know that God will bring us through our situations.

Even more powerful is that God will not bring us through an overwhelming day or a difficult time in our lives and then move to the next person when we are so interconnected through the Holy Spirit. He will always bring us through the crisis we will face in the future. All we have to do is turn to Him and have the faith that, no matter how bad it might get for us in the flesh, yielding to the Spirit of God will always give us the confidence of a better tomorrow.

JAMES 1:2–4

The other day I was talking to someone about exercise. I was telling him about how much I dislike exercising. I do it a lot because I have to maintain a physical regiment that allows me to be healthy. When I was in the army, I had a platoon leader who loved to exercise. When we would do long runs, we had a young soldier who would always fall out of runs. Simply put, he wanted to run his own pace and would always finish, but he just did not want to see how fast he could run five miles. I can't say that I didn't blame him. I would have done the same thing if I didn't fear running the entire thing all over again.

When our run was complete and this young soldier finished, we would all get a lecture about heart from the platoon leader. He would tell us that, without passion, we could not have character. He continued telling us that we have to endure the hardship of physical endurance so we could accomplish our mission, whatever it might be. Having heart and enduring the pain of exercise built a level of character that allowed us to be proud of what we would accomplish through our actions and attitudes as soldiers.

Our faith that God will bring us through the hardships of life is the same way. James writes that faith produces endurance. Without the faith, we would just give up in many circumstances. With the confidence that we can accomplish the current hardship, we will know that our ability to endure will take us to the next issue or hardship. Endurance will give us the stamina to keep moving forward even when it is difficult to take the next step.

We have to endure the hardships because it allows God to complete His work in you. Hardships are the work of Satan, designed to make you upset at God, but God will use it to mold you for His purpose in your life. A work cannot be complete without it. The endurance we face is so we become mature and complete and lack nothing when we are called to accomplish the mission we have in life.

Be assured the challenges will come and you will be faced with temptations, but you will also have opportunity to share in the comfort of God's arms. Faith is not trusting God will remove you from the situation, but trusting He will give you the endurance to get through it. In this statement, "God will never give you more than you can handle," we can see how society misuses it. We can also see what we can use to bring encouragement to those who are hurting because life is overwhelming, but the hands of God are comforting.

CHAPTER 1

SELF-REFLECTION OR SMALL GROUP DISCUSSION QUESTIONS

1. How have you used or seen this statement used to make people feel better about their situation?

2. Did this statement make you or the other person feel better about how God interacts with His people?

3. Were there times in your life that you were tempted? How did you handle it, overcome it, or fall to it?

4. After understanding 1 Corinthians 10:1–21, has your thought of "God will never give you more than you can handle" changed?

5. What does it mean to you when Paul talks about sharing in the communion table?

6. With this knowledge, what does it mean to share in the afflictions of other Christians?

7. How do we share in the comfort of God's arms?

8. How has God prepared you to share His comfort with others through you?

9. What does it mean to have faith that builds endurance?

10. How has God made you mature, complete, and lack nothing through your own trials in life?

CHAPTER 2

Session 3: The Christian Superhero

God cannot give us a happiness and peace apart from Himself, because it is not there, there is no such thing.

—C. S. Lewis

When I was a kid, I wanted to have superpowers. In fact, all the kids I played with as a boy wanted to have superpowers. We pretended to have invisible shields to ward off attacks and force fields and modeled ourselves after the popular superheroes who could fly or shoot laser beams out of their eyes. We could move and run faster than anyone else, especially if you got a new pair of shoes.

As I look at children today, it really isn't any different. They pretend to have superpowers to fight and do great feats. Ironically enough, the superpowers have moved from the internal ability to overcome, as my generation had, to technological abilities of children today.

Even as adults, we sometimes wish we had superpowers. Let's face it. There are times in life where you wish you had special abilities. There are times I still wish I had the power of mind control or the ability to change the weather. When I am sitting in traffic, I wish I could run fast or fly so I would not have to sit in traffic again. The problem is, if we had the power to do life at the speed of light, we probably would just fill our lives with more needless events. The reason we wish we had superpowers is to have a special ability to do more than what we can normally do.

There is something special about the ability to overcome evil through some ingrained power, whether it comes from some celestial indwelling, mutation, or even cryogenically enhanced ability. It would be nice to be the hero that saves the day.

As people of the Christian faith, we have the confidence to know we have the "power of Christ" in us. This superpower is often acknowledged and seldom used. With great confidence, we state, "I can do all things through Christ who strengthens me!" As we begin to tackle the tough task that lays before us, we proclaim this confidence as if it will create a miraculous morphing of our humanity into divine abilities to overcome.

I think it is important to make clear at this point that we are looking at misused statements, not false assertions. I firmly believe that God provides strength to get through the most difficult situations in life, but I do not believe society uses this statement in the way that God intended us to use it.

It is not just church people using this statement as a means of encouragement to get through life's difficult times. People use this assertion in all aspects of their lives. Emotional overload, physical affliction, and spiritual emptiness are all areas where we love to use this concept.

When faced with emotional overload, we use this statement to give ourselves the boost to persevere through the depression, sadness, and anxiety issues. With confidence, we tell ourselves that we can do all things because our strength comes from Christ. Meanwhile we are neglecting to pay attention to the fact that emotional disorders are real and require attention from helping professionals. True emotional and behavioral disorders are not something we can just muscle through. The effects impact not only our well-being but also the comfort and well-being of those around us.

With the same attitude, we repeat this statement to give us the courage in facing treatment plans, go to the next doctor appointment, or even have the strength to help our loved ones get through their own ailments. With confidence, we tell people they can do all things because Christ has given them the strength. Through making that one simple statement, the people we are called to help should receive the power to endure their physical hardships and get past the worry and confusion of their physical ailments.

In the end, we have to face the spiritual effects from this statement. When we are having a difficult time overcoming the emotional overload or the physical ailments, we use this statement for reassurance that God is there for us and He does give us strength in whatever we might face.

We stand in confidence that Philippians 4:13 will be the source of perseverance, courage, and strength through every aspect of our lives. We hope that God will give us these characteristics through Christ who is and always will be there for us. When we fall or fail at the task we face, we become discouraged and begin searching for more answers as to why "God let us down."

When the theory of doing all things through Christ who gives us strength collapses, this can create an overwhelming feeling of God's absence. We place so much trust and faith in a concept that is used so far out of context that we become angry and feel as if our relationship with Christ is not strong enough to overcome.

This attitude is because so many people use the verse outside of its context. When we are facing difficult situations, we cannot just think that God will take over without us seeking Him first. Our discontent in situations will spark dependence on God, but we have to ask ourselves if we need strength or peace in those situations. If we are going to have the Philippians 4:13 strength of Christ, we have to understand what kind of strength God is giving us and how it will help us.

LOOKING AT THE CONTEXT

On the surface, Philippians 4:13 is a solid verse that will inspire us toward strength in overcoming the transgressions, stress, and every aspect of our lives. What many people do not realize is that it is not the type of strength that will give us the power to do all things, including becoming the greatest role model, sports figure, employee of the year, or anything else that our hearts desire.

When Paul wrote this statement, it was in the midst of a passage of thanksgiving. He is not telling them how he was able to overcome any mountain of transgression in his life. He was talking to them about how to be content in what they would face in life. There are three aspects to what Paul was teaching in the entire context of Philippians 4:10–20, and each of the aspects will bring clarity to how God interacts in our life situations.

In the busy society we live in today, there is a great deal of pride with the ability to climb the corporate ladder. We work hard for everything we have. If we do not have what we want, we get frustrated and define ourselves as failures because we have not reached our goals. This lack of contentment leads to restless behavior that becomes damaging in every aspect of our lives.

The simple phrase that we "can do all things through Christ" becomes a phrase we use to push ourselves harder and faster to be the best at what we do and want. Eventually we focus so much on ignoring various aspects of our lives in order to achieve greater things. The attitude of being the greatest then becomes justified in Christ, who will give them strength. We shame ourselves into thinking that failure is not an option because Jesus did not fail at his mission and ministry so we have no right to settle for being less than everything to everyone.

Be Content in Everything

Paul never had the superpower mind-set when he said that Christ gives him strength. Reading verses 10 through 12, we can see where this was furthest from his mind. He is talking about being content with where God has placed him in life. He makes this realization when he says that he has learned to be content in whatever circumstance life brings his way. He uses the word "learned," meaning he has matured in his understanding of God's sovereignty. The mature Christian has learned to be happy with where God has brought him or her and confident in where God is taking him or her.

It is easy to become discontent with where God has you. We lived in a large city at one time, and I had many issues trying to adapt to the urban environment. Every morning I would pray that God would take us out of the city. I was not content with where God had me and how He had me doing ministry. I tried different prayers. Some were prayers that God would allow me to fulfill His will in that city so I could leave. Some were prayers that God would simply allow me to move. I applied for jobs all over the nation and would not receive any responses or interviews.

Finally I made the decision that, no matter how much I did not like where I was at, I was going to be content in the ministry that God placed in my path. The first thing that happened is that my ministry flourished. I had a different attitude toward the people and the difficulties in ministry. After a few months of being surrendered to God, He provided a way out of the circumstance I was in.

Sometimes we say we are doing something for God but kicking and screaming the entire time. It is as if we say, "Yes, God, I will follow you, but only when I feel comfortable." We fail to remember that the most uncomfortable of times is exactly when God is shaping, teaching, or growing us for the next ministry opportunity we have. It does not mean we do not look for those opportunities. It means we faithfully do what we have to where we are called to do it without griping and complaining.

Being content with God does not always deal with where or what we are doing for God. Sometimes it is being content with how much we have. Paul expands on this in verse 12 when he writes, "I know both how to have a little, and I know how to have a lot." People desire many of the possessions in which they place value. Overloading themselves with the things their heart desires, these people begin to gather possessions outside their means, ending up in deeper distress.

We have to remember that, when God blesses us with various things, accepting them and gaining them within moderation allows us to appreciate the blessing from God. In some respect, this becomes addictive behavior that looks for how we can get more of something instead of the behaviors that allow us to be content in what we already have. Just like the story above, we have to be content before God will trust us with more.

The other point in having a little or a lot as well as being well-fed or hungry is God's ability to provide for our needs at the time. Only through our experiences with God do we have the confidence in God's ability to provide what we need every time. We might not have everything we want, but God provides exactly what we need.

When I started in ministry, we did not have anything. Now when I say that, I do not mean we were poor, but I mean we were living in a hotel room. I had just gotten a job, and we were waiting for my pay to kick in so we could catch up with bills that were behind and save enough money for a deposit on a house. This experience was humbling, to say the least. Our youngest son had just been born, so five of us were living in a hotel room, trying to make ends meet.

In an effort to get some extra money coming in, I began to talk with local funeral homes to preach services for people who did not have a pastor. I remember how excited we were to get the first call. This was our chance to get out of the hotel and into a small apartment, if I could get enough calls. This also brought on a great deal of stress. The extra money would be a huge help, but I did not own a suit or dress shoes.

We thought about it for a while and then made the decision to purchase an inexpensive suit. This would allow me to stand in front of the people and look presentable. I also had my military low quarters that I had not shined yet, so I could wear those with the suit. The thought was that if we could get a few of the funeral checks, I would be able to buy shoes.

It has been decisions like these that change the way I look at ministry. I was never someone who went straight from high school with a clear focus on ministry. I can associate with Paul in the case of knowing what it is like to have a lot and a little. My wife and I know what it is like to skip a meal so we can make sure our kids eat, and there are many people in the world that also know what it is like to skip a meal.

Have you ever been hungry? I don't mean the type of hungry because you are on a diet or too busy to eat, but the kind of hungry that leaves you famished because you don't have the capability to get food. Paul knows this feeling and reflects it to the people with an attitude of contentment. He is taking a moment to thank the church for helping him and showing concern for his well-being. They understand that ministry cannot be sustained without the help of other people.

As he thanks them, he is not asking for more, but he is showing his confidence in God's ability to provide because of his faithfulness. Once again, he writes he has "learned," but this time he has learned the secret of contentment. We can look at this as the maturing process, but by saying he has learned the secret, he is telling the people that not everyone knows how to be content.

We have to pay special attention to the times someone has learned something when it involves our relationship with God. Cracking the code of God's blessings is a very special thing that should always be taken seriously. Paul has learned a secret when it comes to being content because a process of maturity had to take place in order for him to understand contentment while others have not figured out the secret.

When we have a secret, an intimate acquaintance takes place between the secret holder and the receiver. We know and understand something that others have not figured out yet. People love to have secrets. It is natural for all of us to want to know something that others don't. When this happens, we are either excited to share with them and teach them something new, or we hold it close and do not tell anyone.

In the case of relationship with God, there should be no secrets because that will hinder the growth and development of other brothers and sisters. When Paul writes that he has learned the secret of contentment, he is writing that he understands an intimate detail about being content that so many other people do not know. The use is not simply having the knowledge but having it with the intention of teaching.

Discontent comes in abundance. One of the things I like about the military is that, no matter how discontent I can become with my duty location, I know I will be able to move in a few years, sometimes to a location that is better and other times not so good. Ways we are discontent range from food, jobs, and other people, and the list goes on. Very rarely do people bask in contentment found in Christ because they are so consumed with their discontent in life.

When we become discontent, we find ourselves focused in things of the world, and we are focused on worldly items instead of heavenly things. Understanding where God has us and being patient enough to learn why He has us somewhere has a great deal of influence when it comes to being content. Oftentimes we are looking at the next step in the rung and worried about climbing the ladder so fast that we fail to be familiar with our current rung in the ladder of life. Using life's situation as a stepping-stone to an ultimate goal discounts the sovereignty of God because it places trust in our own ability to get through life instead of His ability to bring us through situations.

The Secret of Contentment

This is where we understand the concepts found in verse 13 and 14. While we pull this verse for strength, we have to understand a few phrases in these two short sentences. Outside of God's grace, it is impossible to be content. I cannot count how many times I hear the phrase, "If I only had …" The point they are making is the feeling that happiness would be achieved through obtaining items.

It is easy for people to believe, if they could only get the next qualification, others would respect them in the community. There is a fine balance between underqualified, qualified, and overqualified. People will look at where other people are and want to do or participate in the things they were doing to get there. As a result, a desperate search and effort to seek the qualifications of a certain status ensues. Unsatisfied people will work hard to have the same as others, only to leave behind the plan God has for their lives.

When this happens, we are literally all over the place. We are trying to become a jack-of-all-trades but a master at none. Our basic knowledge of many subjects makes us smart and able to hold a conversation in many circles, but not knowledgeable enough to be recognized by any desired professional community. We begin to lack direction. We desire fame but don't realize we set goals on too narrow of a path to become an expert because we are willing to follow every trail in the process of achieving our dreams.

Eventually we have to understand, in order to reach our goals, we must first become an expert in one particular area. At that point we find contentment because our focus was not on everyone else, but on God's goal for our lives. We are only able to achieve this one goal through slowing down and being patient.

Paul uses the word "through" in this passage for us to understand the first step in the secret of contentment. The word implies the means in which we accomplish tasks. Who knows if we will ever become famous, but knowing God's plan for us certainly causes us to be focused. If God allows us to be famous, it would be through focused dedication and hard work. Paul is saying that we can endure unrest in all things because Christ is the means he receives strength.

This is not a secret formula for having greater powers, but it's an enigma to enduring the things that breed discontent. We are all over the place in life, hoping to have the secret formula for happiness. Having bigger bank accounts, being around more people, increasing the size of our house, or winning the lottery all serve as areas we feel might provide happiness. The secret, though, is not in the tangibles, but in the heart.

We have to remember that the tangibles are His blessing because we have been content in what He has already given us. Happiness is found through God, not through the blessing. When we find contentment through God, we receive His strength. This is a concept that has gone by the wayside in a world that is filled with entitlement attitudes. If we feel like we are entitled to God's blessing, we will never be content with what He has or even is giving us. We will always want and search for something better.

When we find contentment in God and not the blessing, we then find strength to overcome any situation, even if the circumstance is failure. This does not mean that we should just wait for life to come to us or for God to give us everything the world says we need to hold various positions. This means we find patience in where we are now and try to grow as much as possible in that moment so we are ready to move when God blesses us with further opportunity.

Patience takes a lot of strength and restraint. God gives us the power to be content in our achievements or failures. Some of the greatest inventors and notable people in society did not achieve greatness because they were moving in different directions for their lives, but they were focused. We would not have electricity if it were not for a focused effort. Light bulbs, music, and all the things we enjoy in modern technology are a product of people focused on one goal. When they failed, they learned. And when they learned, they improved. The strength to persevere in the midst of failure comes from being content with success and failure.

Spiritual success and failure is a shared responsibility. As believers, we have to have both the concept of one body and shared success and failure. Society is closing in on the Christian belief system as an irrational, intolerant faith group that looks toward preaching and judging more than loving. Churches fight about whose ministry turf belongs to whom and who has the best programs to reach the community. Simply bringing people into the church is not good enough anymore.

If we are going to point people toward the strength of Christ or even help strengthen people in Christ, we can no longer be churches, but the church. Just as the church shared in Paul's hardship, we take that example. It is not feeling proud because we gave to the special missions offering or provided the neighbor a ride to worship. It is not even ensuring the neighborhood kids come to VBS during the summer. We have to understand it is all of those things that share in the brotherhood and sisterhood of the Christian faith.

I see so many people who are proud of what they have done to help point people toward Jesus. Any time we have the opportunity to praise God for what He has done in the life of another person should be celebrated. When you have an opportunity to share your faith and testimony with others, this is celebrated in heaven and should be hailed in the church. When a new church starts, it should be observed that another resource has entered into the community, not considered as business competition that might take away from the offering plate at your church.

When I entered into ministry, I was told to do what God called me to do, regardless of the opposition. I have heard stories all over America about opposition even within denominational competition. In one case, I heard of a pastor criticizing another of the same denomination for planting a church within ten miles of his church. Pastors all over have loads of reasons why there shouldn't be any competition for their church. Instead of looking toward kingdom growth, they should look toward congregational growth. This is dangerous because it changes the church's missional mandate toward a business model focused on appeasing the community social needs as opposed to their own spiritual need.

When we talk about sharing in the success and pain of the church, it means we are not creating pain for another church but praying for their success in fulfilling the part of the body they are called to. It does not matter that your neighbor might be going to another church as much as the fact that they are connected to a group of believers. The church today has been so lost in building their own success that they have failed to realize the hurt and pain of other churches and their congregations.

There are churches that see others are in hardship and make every attempt to save them, but for the most part, we are afraid to show adversity to the community because that weakness requires possible surrender. Instead of showing the willingness to change, they silently fade away in the name of tradition. We should not capitalize in the midst of our brothers' and sisters' hardships but share with them in their want.

We as a body of believers have to understand that God gifts each church in a way that will allow them to grow. To look at one part of the community of believers and say they are not worthy to be in the same area is like saying your fingernail is not worthy of being part of the finger because it is not like the rest of the finger. It does not make sense to shun people because we do not understand their purpose in the eyes of God.

Being a church body that says you can execute the program better because you have more resources is discounting what God intended for the church. Instead of making a statement that focuses on doing something better, use the resources you were blessed with to help the other church grow and develop their program. To start programs for the sake of having them will take away from the hurting church that God might be growing through the ministry He gave them.

In return, these hardships, coupled with the competition, bleeds into discipleship of the body. Pastors who see the church across the street or a few blocks away as competition only breeds hardship and contempt (1 Cor. 12:21–26). When a high level of contempt is created within the community of believers, not only does one part of the body suffer, but also the entire body suffers. This is an example on a greater scale when looking at sharing in the hardship, but we also have to view at how sharing in hardship can damage others within the congregation.

Individuals who are suffering from discontent have a challenge in front of them. While many pastors will preach that a church is the place for the broken to be healed, some pay no attention to others' needs as much as they come to church to have their needs met. If we go before our church family with the attitude that our needs must be met, we fail to see that church is about the advancement of the entire kingdom of God, not just the individual child of God. We will look at this principle closer in chapter 4. For this section, it is important for us to focus on caring for the hurting.

While it is difficult to be content and suffering is never a pleasant experience, the secret to contentment is through the strength that God provides. Relying on anything else can lead to further dissatisfaction. As part of the body, our job is to be the hands and work of God in a way that can bring help to the hardship that people are facing. Through Christ, we can and do all things because we find strength to be content in all circumstances. We have to surrender our pride and be prepared to receive help by those whom God has placed in our lives.

GOD WILL ALWAYS SUPPLY YOUR NEEDS

Each person has two things in life. Before you begin to think "death and taxes," look at it from a different perspective. Death and taxes bring very little contentment in life. Let's look at this from the viewpoint of being content. There are two aspects we should look at: what we want and what we need. Often we put our wants before our needs in life. This is shown through the material desires of an instant gratification world.

Wants are the things in our lives that are not needed for survival, but they are nice to have and bring temporary pleasure. Note I said temporary pleasure because, when we want something and finally get it, oftentimes we enjoy it for a short while and then put it in a box and stow it away in an attic or garage until we have the next yard sale. Then we put it on a table with all the rest of the "wants" for people who might want it more.

If we add up how much money we spend on all the things we want in life, we might find our main point of debt, credit card bills, and all the other messes we get put in. However, there are things we want with all our hearts that will bring us happiness but never get. Working in ministry, I have found people who want things so badly that they ask me to avoid praying for God's will in obtaining it and directly pray for the person to receive the desired want.

When we begin to pray for our wants that are outside of God's will, we have lost focus on what we need and become refocused on what we want. This takes away from the lasting contentment found in God and focuses on how we become content through things of this world. Eventually our needs are secondary to our wants, and ultimately they will take a higher position to receive. The unfortunate part of this is that our return on investment is low because it only brings temporary joy and low reimbursable return.

This leads to the tricky business of discerning wants and needs. Some aspects of wants and needs are hard to determine, and others are easy. For example, if I go for an afternoon snack, I really want cookies, but what I need is an apple. There is an easy designation between the two. However, it is more difficult when we need a dependable car but want the most expensive luxury vehicle we can get a loan approved for. When people dangle the money in front of you, it is easy to take the cash and get what we want. There are businesses all over the world who prey on people's wants instead of their needs. These organizations offer money, status, loyalty, and anything they can get for people to upgrade their lifestyle while downgrading their livelihood.

When our needs are fulfilled, we find a different kind of contentment in life. We have security, and along with that is the ability to have hope for our future. God provides a different kind of contentment when we look at the difference between wants and needs. Once we take the time to discern the difference between what we want (temporary happiness) found in social status and desire, we lose sight of what we need (eternal happiness) found in spiritual status and desire. Praying for our needs almost always allows us to make wise decisions in determining what we want. Oftentimes when we focus on the need and bring that to God's will, He will give us not only what we need but also what we want.

King Solomon is a perfect example of this concept (1 Kings 3). God asked King Solomon what he wanted, and King Solomon asked for wisdom to lead God's people. God blessed King Solomon with wisdom but gave him everything he could have asked for as well. In this case, Solomon asked for what he needed, but God gave him not only what he needed but also what he wanted.

In our world today, we have to discern what will make us eternally content with life. When we earnestly pray for something, God will give it to us if it is within His will and we truly need it. Our faithfulness with the needs will reciprocate the blessing to receive some of our wants.

When we have contentment in where God has us and is taking us, we can have the confidence that He will supply the resources to get us there. Often we look at what we do not have as inhibitors to achieving our calling instead of opportunities to receive blessings in order to give blessings to others. Pride will also get in the way of our desire to ask for what we need. We do this for many reasons. Sometimes we do not think people will understand why we are asking for it. Other times we are afraid to ask because of what we assume other people might think.

Regardless of why we do not ask for things, we have to remember, if God called us to the ministry, we must first ask Him for the tools to accomplish the task. Second, we must understand that He will not give us some tools until we learn how to use the ones we have. Finally, we have to understand what tools we need to do the ministry instead of what tools we want to do the ministry.

Once we take a methodological approach to answering God's call, we begin to understand the hardships we face in life are preparing us to help others. Once this happens, we take two approaches in our view of God:

1. We depend on God more and more to get us through a situation. This is always important because God is the giver and sustainer of life. When times are difficult, the dependence on God to provide will always reap blessing through answered prayer.

2. This approach is seen more often when it comes to dealing with hardship in life. Instead of depending on God for the strength to be content in life's situation, we become even more dissatisfied with God. We reject the notion that He might answer prayer or the thought that He is intimately involved in our lives. At this point, you might question why atrocities happen to God's people, and I will address that in chapter 7 at a deeper level. We have to remember that God is intimately involved in everyone's life and His goal is to provide for His people. When we face hardship, it is not because God does not care as much as Satan trying to make us believe He doesn't care.

In Philippians 4:15–20, Paul expands on the prospect of God supplying his needs to do ministry. This is where we can grasp the thought that God will always supply our needs. Two concepts that can be pulled from this passage is that the gift blesses the giver as much as the receiver and God can provide beyond your means.

In verse 17, Paul makes an interesting statement, "Not that I seek the gift, but I seek the profit that is increasing to your account." As mentioned before, society is looking at what their personal gain might be from something that they miss the blessing it can provide for other people. In fact, when we talk about projects and outreach events, we ask ourselves what is in it for us. We offer free trinkets, food, and gifts, and the list goes on. Paul, however, reverses this thought and prompts us to change our attitude from "what's in it for me" to "what's in it for you."

We should accept gifts from others because it provides blessings for the giver just as much as it does for the receiver. We feel good when we are able to help someone in need. Imagine the greatest gift you gave someone or even a time when you have helped someone. Think of how proud you felt because you had the opportunity to bless someone else's life. Transfer that into the thought process of blessing people every day in your Christian walk.

When you are too proud to accept gifts from other people when you are facing hardship, not only does this take away your own blessing; it removes the profit of blessing for the other giver. We do not seek the gift, as Paul writes, but we see the increasing of blessing in the other person's life.

When we focus on the life that meets our needs more than our wants, we make decisions on how to provide service to others. Instead of taking the social status in the moment, we chose to invest in the life of another person that will ultimately pay dividends in eternity. Our choice to follow the settle nudging of the Lord allows the Spirit to well up within us and overflow into the lives of others.

This leads into the second point. Just as much as we can gain eternal contentment through the ministry of others, which exercises the point Paul made in verse 19, it is important to understand through faithfulness and contentment that Christ will provide for us beyond our own means. There is a big difference between living beyond your means and God providing beyond your means.

God providing beyond your means relates to God's ability to bless you with things that you never expected nor could afford. Many people can't afford a new car, but God blesses them beyond their means through others. What's more is that, when He blesses us beyond our means, He provides for a way to sustain that blessing. This is how we know if God blessed us beyond our means or we have overextended ourselves.

When we are able to sustain the blessing, we know that God has blessed us beyond our means. When we are not able to sustain the blessing, we realize that God did not give us the blessing, but we took it for our own fulfilled desire. When we reach the level of spiritual maturity that we find comfort in God's grace, we realize that He will bless us beyond our means. This is because, just as we are limited in in riches in this world, God is without limit.

There is no way for God to live outside His means, despite what we think might be too small or big an issue we completely understand, as Paul relates in verse 19, "God will supply all your needs according to his riches in glory in Christ Jesus." By eliminating God from our situations, we are implying that God cannot provide for us the way we can provide for ourselves.

Our contentment is found in God. The supply of all our needs is received from God. When we feel that all avenues have failed us, we can have the confidence that God has never nor will ever fail us. We want plenty of things, but we have to remember that what we want and what we need are two different things. If we seek what we need and depend on God for those needs, you will do all things through Christ who gives strength.

What Should We Use Instead

Looking at the context for the statement, "I can do all things through Christ who strengthens me," Paul was not relaying a message of being a superhero, or we would have extraordinary strength to accomplish great feats. Instead he was talking about the need for people to find contentment because God provides all our needs. This translates into a very important aspect of Christian living where we can depend on God to care for us without being selfish and greedy.

It is not about asking for what we need as much as it is being content with what we have. When this happens, Christ is glorified in our lives because we recognize the power and strength of God to sustain us in our every need. It is, however, important for us to understand what we should use to be and provide encouragement to others when they are facing emotional, physical, and spiritual pain in their lives.

Emotional Strife

So many people face emotional loss when they think about what their expectations for life were when they started off in the world. Like so many people when we think about what our expectations are for the future and where we are not, it can sometimes disappoint us or even create a level of emotional strife that causes hopelessness and suicidal thoughts on one end. And the other is an emotional turmoil that makes us dissatisfied and moody. It is not regret but unfulfilled expectations for the future that cause us to make irrational decisions that can lead to divorce, discontentment, anger, and frustration. The decision we make in life can greatly affect how we emotional react to situations.

The woman who is afraid of not having a child gets pregnant by a man she believes she loves but is more in love with the thought of having kids than the notion of having true love is a perfect example of expectations. The man who believed he would be rich by his midforties and made a lot of bad investments that caused him to lose money instead of growing his savings is another example of bad decisions. However, sometimes these expectations can be positive too.

When I was young, I wanted to earn my doctorate; however, my life did not take me down a road that lead to doctoral-level education. My expectations were not being met, and I was disappointed because of it. When I was in my late thirties, I realized I was not achieving any goals for my life, so I went back to school to do something about it.

Our expectations can either weaken us or give us strength and courage to face the challenging road ahead. I saw a lot of people who dropped out of school while trying to chase their goals of education, but I have also seen many others who used their adversity to achieve more than they ever dreamed of. How comfortable we are is based on how much peace we have in life's situations and the direction we are going in our lives.

As Jesus is preparing his disciples for the death and crucifixion, he begins to teach them about the gift of peace (John 14:27). In this singular verse, he makes three promises for the disciples as he prepares them for what was about to happen. He has just finished telling them about the Holy Spirit in the previous verse. Christ refers to the Holy Spirit as the Counselor that will teach them all things and remind them of everything he has taught them (John 114:26). This is relevant because Jesus is going to transition into a teaching about peace in his bodily absence.

He begins in verse 27 with the statement, "Peace I leave with you." This is where understanding the role of the Holy Spirit comes into play. While Christ states to the disciples that He is leaving peace with them, we can have the confidence that Christ is leaving peace with all of His people.

For some who have not met their life's expectations, they lack peace. In a few cases, they don't know where to get the peaceful presences of God. Everything they had built in their adult life on was based on the hustle and bustle of life's demands. When they come to the point of calling for help, life has simply demanded too much from them, and they have no place else to turn.

When Christ is talking about leaving peace with His disciples, He is referring to an inner place of tranquility that cannot be experienced through any other means. Christ is not just leaving peace behind with us as an item we are supposed to keep watch on until He returns. He is leaving it for us to experience.

In the next section of this verse, he says, "My peace I give to you." This means He is giving it to us as a gift. Christ knows He has to pay the price for our peace. He knows that, through His aguish and painful experiences, we will be able to experience God's peace in life. We have to understand that peace is not a concept that is gained from anything other than God.

Our society often mistakes financial security for peace. We believe that life will bring peace as long as wc provide for our family and do the things that society implies will bring us happiness and contentment. As a society, we experience false peace every day. We often think, if we only went the extra mile for our boss or established good boundaries in our relationships, we will experience peace. Christ does not—nor has ever—promise peace through the things of this world. In order for us to experience the tranquility of the Holy Spirit, we have to understand the peace that Christ gives us is not what the world gives.

This leads into the second promise Christ makes in this passage. He tells the disciples, "I do not give to you as the world gives." This means the peace that Christ gives is true peace. A divine peace can only come from the Holy Spirit. When I pray for people who are facing emotional overload, I will often ask God to give them a "peace that passes all understanding."

Too often people put their stock in the false peace of this world. Once this peace fails them or they are on the brink of an emotional breakdown, they feel as if the world has failed them, or they turn to God and believe He has failed them. We have to remember that divine peace only comes from God. A level of tranquility takes place that no one will ever be able to understand.

Every day people make phone calls to hotlines designed to help people find peace. Oftentimes this is done in desperation after they believe they do not have anywhere to turn. In the midst of emotional strife, they call Christian hotlines as a last resort. In many cases, the person on the other end of the line listens to the stories of the hurting and will guide them to an understanding of God's peace, which allows them to find future hope in the circumstance they are facing. This future hope allows hurting souls to experience tranquility despite what they might be facing in life. This does not mean that life's situations will magically disappear, but it means we can be okay with God's hand protecting us through the emotional strife.

When Christ gives us the peace he leaves through the Holy Spirit, a peace that is not of this world, we have the confidence of his third promise in this verse. Christ instructs them that their "heart must not be troubled or fearful." Telling someone this is much easier said than putting into practice. We have to remember that God does not call us to put peace into practice, but to receive His peace so we may experience what His faithful arms have to offer.

When facing the emotional strife of life, the thought we can overcome it because Christ gives us strength can give us a false sense of healing when, in fact, we can have peace so our hearts are not experiencing stress or anxiety over situations. People who believe they can get through issues without professional help fail to realize one key aspect to God's ability in the intervention process. We have to understand that He gifts and prepares people as His instrument for emotional healing.

When Christ says He is leaving and giving us His peace, He is stating that He will give us a peace that passes all understanding. This peace comes from depending on God to get through the situation. He does give us strength to be content in the situation, but most of all, He gives us peace to face the situation with a level of tranquility. For us to put our faith and hope in anything outside of someone who depends on God to provide that peace is just as hazardous as the false hope we have by gaining peace from material items and relationships in this world.

Physical Affliction

Sometimes I have the privilege to work with wounded warriors. For those who do not know, this is the name society has given to military members who have permanent emotional or physical wounds. In most cases, their wounds are a result of their undying service to our country. These men and women face every day with physical and emotional affliction, and they continually amaze me.

In many cases these warriors are the pictures of health before their injury, but through their battle-scarred circumstances, they become someone new. Some handle situations with the optimistic outlook of life's blessings, but others are consumed with what could have been or what they used to be that they are devastated and lose their zeal for what life has in store for them.

You can only imagine how devastating it is for some of these warriors to lose their identity in the midst of the battlefield. Even in the midst of physical change, the emotional quandaries begin to set in. They recount the trauma of the battlefield, they question their future success, and they learn a new way of life that includes certain accommodations.

In some cases the physical affliction triggers emotional strife that prevents them from having the will to go down the long road of recovery. However, for some, the story does not stop at the pity they initially feel in the hospital bed. Many of these warriors are pointed toward hope-focused recovery that involves a spiritual aspect that reflects on how God can use them in their new self.

When talking to some of these wounded warriors, they attribute most of their will to recover from the encouragement that chaplains, pastors, and people of faith provide for them on a daily basis. Some say they would have never gotten out of the hospital bed if it weren't for the encouragement of others who helped them see past their circumstances. For others, they would have never known what it was like to have a relationship with Christ, and most of all, they would have never overcome the emotional and physical affliction they face daily.

As you read this chapter, you might have been thinking about 2 Corinthians 12:9–10 and the fact it talks about strength through Christ just like Philippians 4:13. It is important to understand the venues in which Paul is speaking. Philippians 4:13 is talking about being content in all circumstances. If you will remember, I did say that Christ gives us strength to overcome situations. Looking at this verse, we can see that we are empowered when we are weak.

Paul is writing about the thorn in his flesh that was given to him so he would not exalt himself more than he should (2 Cor. 12:7). He writes that he pleaded with God three times to remove his thorn. While many people belabor what the thorn was, we will simply believe it was something that weakened him or caused some level of physical setback in his ministry.

Through Paul's pleading, God speaks to him and makes two profound statements. First, "My grace is sufficient for you." On the surface, it might look like God is telling Paul that His forgiveness from salvation is sufficient for life. Grace in this case extends beyond salvation and relates to the mercy and kindness that affords the joy and peace we can experience in life. When we experience true grace, we have the ability to experience joy and, most of all, peace in the physical affliction we face, no matter what it might be.

Helping professionals, especially chaplains, are able to show wounded warriors the mercy and kindness of God that allow them to experience God's joy and peace in the midst of their physical affliction. Without God working through the ministry of the others, these warriors would never know what God's joy and peace really felt like.

God has full intention to use each of us as an instrument of grace to His people. Through those who have and share the peace of God, people might know what a peace that passes all understanding feels like. As a Christian, all have experienced the minimal point of grace, which is salvation, and when we have faced life circumstances, we have experienced peace. Some of these wounded warriors' physical affliction can just as easily overtake their willingness to recover, but when they allow the Holy Spirit to take over, they have an opportunity to experience a peace-giving power to push through any affliction.

The second statement God speaks is, "For power is perfected in weakness." This does not mean that we gain a supernatural power to accomplish any task, but Christ is our source of power. When "power is perfected," this means that Christ is perfected in our weakness. We do not chase after physical power in the midst of our weakness, but the perfected power of the spirit. The very essence that allows us to face the day with joy and peace is perfected power from God.

When the power manifests itself in our weakness, we are able to display Christ in our lives. Our testimony is developed because we are able to overcome unnatural circumstances in our lives outside of our own knowledge and understanding. If you have ever been in a situation that was so physically overwhelming that you did not have any idea on how you would overcome the situation but somehow you were able to, you have experienced the grace and perfect power of Christ in the midst of your weakness.

Weakness does not constitute surrender; it magnifies submission. When I think about surrender, it reminds me of giving up. When we surrender to God, yes, we have given up trying to do things on our own and have allowed God to take over. This is a great concept, but God does not ask us to walk away from situations as if we have no part in the process. On the other hand, when we magnify submission, we are recognizing God has greater control over the situation and He is in charge. When we recognize someone is in charge, we listen carefully to his or her direction and make every attempt to follow that path for the task that has to be done.

Power is perfected in submission, not surrender. It is our ability to understand that, through our weakness, God will give us perfect direction. Realizing that God is in full control and being able to listen to His direction will allow us to complete each task with perfection in the eyes of the God.

Some of the wounded warriors I know who have had life-changing experiences with God no longer talk about how much they are can't do but how well they are able to recover from their emotional and physical setbacks. What was once a personal competition on how much endurance they could build to run the fastest or furthest has now turned into a personal competition of how much they endure to learn how to walk and run. Through God, these warriors understand the perfect power of Christ's grace because they have submitted to the Lord that has and always will bring them through life's toughest situations.

If we feel sorry for ourselves over physical afflictions, we are missing the testimony that God has given us. Paul says he will "most gladly boast all the more about weaknesses, so that Christ's power may reside" in him. When we give a testimony about how Christ has played a role in our lives, we are putting Him at the forefront of everything we do. Gladly boasting about Christ is being a witness for Christ. When we boast about Him in our weaknesses, we understand that Christ is the primary source for strength in the trials we face. We find pleasure in these trials because of what Christ can and will do in our lives.

Verse 10 begins with finding pleasure in the midst of "weaknesses, insults, catastrophes, persecutions, and in pressures." Why does he take pleasure? When we are weak, Christ in us is the strongest. In the midst of our weakness, we have an automatic tendency to reduce ourselves in search of what will reflect strength. When Christ is in our lives, we depend on Him so much for everything that every ounce of our being reflects Christ to others.

Some wounded warriors have a great deal of weakness in the muscles that help them walk and achieve the goals they had for their lives. They are forced to strengthen the appropriate muscles so they are able to walk with prosthetics. In the same respect, we have to exercise our willingness to submit to God in order for His perfection to show in and through us.

This can only be exercised through the trials and tribulations we face in life. God uses these moments as teachable times where we can understand how helpless life can leave us. Understanding that we are predominately weak in every aspect of our lives brings to light the power of God. While many think they have control over their situations, a major physical affliction can reveal just how helpless we truly are. In the 2 Corinthians passage, we learn that events in our lives are part of the testimony that we are weak and, in many cases, helpless, but God is strong. He will always give the joy and peace that perfects our situation, regardless of how in control we might feel or want to be.

Feeling in control of our physical affliction gives us the false hope that we can handle the situation without God. Once this happens, we do not fall back on Christ. We look for the solutions ourselves. This futile search will always produce ideas but will never give a lasting strength to overcome physical affliction. When we are faced with physical affliction, we have to understand that it is not that we can do all things through Christ who strengthens us, but we can have the joy and peace of Christ because of his strength perfected in us.

Spiritual Courage

Faith that God will provide His perfect peace and strength in our lives creates spiritual crises in may people. While we know that God has brought us through so many situations, human nature always questions the situation. It is natural for us to ask: What if this is the time that God is not there? What if He does not bring us through this time?

I remember going through air assault school when I was younger. Once we got to the repel phase of the school, we would have to learn certain techniques and then put them into practice. I always wanted to go second despite how many people wanted to go first. My reasoning was simple. If the rope on the tower were rigged wrong, the first person would find out the hard way. The more people who went in front of me increased the odds of the rope giving out if it were to give at any point in the training. Going second, in my mind, was the safest position to be in when doing such dangerous operations. Regardless of the position I went in, there were days we repelled all day long. The heavy schedule meant I had to have faith in many factors:

1. I had to believe the cadre rigged the ropes correctly.
2. I had to have faith the person at the bottom of the rope would be paying attention should I have any issues.
3. I had to have faith in my equipment and the knowledge that I tied my rig correct.
4. I had to have faith in the guy who was inspecting my equipment.

Without believing in every aspect of the repel, I would not be able to walk to the top of the tower and successfully complete my task.

When searching for spiritual courage, there is only one person we have to place our faith in, the Holy Spirit. We have to trust that God will give attention to every aspect of our lives. Unlike the faith and trust needed to hook up to the rappel rope where it was spread out to several factors, God is the only source we have to place our trust in. Once we do that, we can experience spiritual courage that transcends beyond what we could ever imagine.

Faith and trust in the Holy Spirit comes from recognizing the experiences we have had in the past. When God brings us through situations in the past, we have the confidence that He will always bring us through the most difficult of situations. This inspires an excitement that is incomparable to anything we would ever experience.

Overcoming our fears and anxiety with faith is what Paul writes Timothy in his second letter. Paul ensures Timothy understands the spirit that dwells within all Christians and constantly reminds ourselves that God's spirit is not something that gives fear but has a life-giving principle that includes courage to face our fears.

When facing our fears, we have to be fired up for God. Paul writes to Timothy, reminding him to "keep ablaze the gift of God that is in [him]" (2 Tim. 1:6). We have to be able to hold a zeal for God that is like no other.

We do not get this zeal from sitting around and waiting on the anointing of the Holy Spirit, like the disciples in the upper room. We get this anointing when we find salvation in the Lord.

At the point, the Holy Spirit comes upon us when we are reborn in Christ (Matt. 18:3; John 3:3). We are made new, and we receive the gift of the Holy Spirit. This gift develops and matures when we surround ourselves with the right people to provide encouragement and growth in our spiritual lives. Having the right people to guide and instruct us is a key principle to having spiritual courage.

Just as I gained courage to repel off the tower because someone went before me, we can have courage to face trials when we know others have faced the same spiritual hurdles. The soldier who went down the rope before me had one thing I did not, two minutes of experience that I had not dealt with yet. His or her ability to go down the rope right before me did give me the confidence that the rope would not break. When we have people around us who are on fire for God, despite what they might be facing in life, we are empowered to be on fire for God as well. We have to set our gifts ablaze through dedication to the Holy Spirit, and in return we will have the spiritual courage to overcome.

When it comes to spiritual courage, we have to understand that God's Spirit in us is not afraid, but we are (2 Tim. 1:7a). The absence of fear negates the need for faith. Without fear, we have no way of displaying courage, and without that, we have no way to show our trust in something more powerful than we are. We have to ask ourselves which of the two will prevail in our lives, fear or faith.

If we remain consumed by fear, we will never be able to see how our relationship with Christ will bring us through situations. We would never be able to experience the peace that God provides in every situation. Being overwhelmed by fear prevents us from seeing and trusting what God has in store for us.

If I had been consumed by fear on the repel tower, I would not be able to turn and push off for repelling. The emotional factor of mortality often takes over, and we are stunned by the prospect that what we have to face might take our lives. When it comes to spiritual fear, we begin to question what we believe. The fear that God might leave us or is not interested in us prevents us from having faith. We start to live our lives in a way that negates God from every circumstance and situation. This is often seen in people who lose a loved one or feel they have been treated badly by others in religious forums.

When faith consumes us, we have the courage to face each fear with the confidence that the Holy Spirit will guide and protect us. While this might sound like a bold statement, imagine the things we do, both spiritually and worldly. How do some people have the confidence to repel from the tower while others fear even climbing the flight of stairs? Many attribute this to a chemical desire for adrenaline or the courage they hold within. For Christians, it is the drive of the Holy Spirit. We do not have to worry about what tomorrow will bring in the scheme of eternity. If tomorrow brings physical death, we have gained eternity.

When our faith allows us to overcome life's obstacles, we no longer have spiritual emptiness because we feel and experience God in every trial faced. God has not given us a fearful spirit because God is not a fearful God. He has created all that is within us and all that surrounds us. He halts and allows us to experience life as He sees appropriate, in a way that helps us grow emotionally, physically, and, most of all, spiritually.

When we yield to our own fears and allow the Holy Spirit to grow and develop in us, we begin to experience power, love, and sound judgment (2 Tim. 1:7b). These attributes are those of the body through power, the soul through love, and sound judgment through the mind. The development of all human life is the total being of body, soul, and mind. The spirit that God placed in us is reflected of His good nature through a holistic empowerment.

In our body, we receive the power of Christ to be content and endure the hardship that life might bring our way. In the soul, we understand that God is love, and through Him, we show this divine love to others. Finally in the mind, God is the author of wisdom. Without His wisdom, we would not be able to make decisions that help us overcome fear, transgression, and attacks from the enemy.

Without God in every aspect of our lives, we do not have the ability to endure all that life will place in our paths. God has designed the Holy Spirit to be the counselor and empowerment for His people. Satan might scavenge all over this earth, trying to destroy humanity's relationship with God (1 Peter 5:8), but the only progress he is able to make is that which we allow. This is because, while God allows these trials to come our way, we decide to run to or from Him.

We can see through a study of this statement that God did not give us supernatural powers to do anything we want to do, but He gave us an indwelling of peace that He has conquered the world. Instead of saying we can do all things through Christ who strengthens us, we should say we could face all things through the peace that Christ has given us through His Holy Spirit. We always have to remember that Christ has already overcome the world. All we have to do is receive the peace He gives so we can face tomorrow because of what Christ has already done on the cross.

CHAPTER 2

SELF-REFLECTION OR SMALL GROUP DISCUSSION QUESTIONS

1. How have you used this statement to provide encouragement for someone to get through a difficult time in his or her life?

2. Where have you seen this statement used in society today?

3. What does Philippians 4:13 mean to you personally?

4. When looking at contentment, what areas do you struggle with being content in?

5. Have you ever been in a chaotic situation but still found peace with where you were?

6. How does sharing in each other's hardship apply to your life?

   a. Your small group's growth?
   b. Your church?
   c. Your community?

7. How are we blessed by giving just as much, if not more than, being the recipient of a blessing?

8. How have you been blessed as a giver?

9. Has God ever blessed you with something outside of your means?

10. What does it mean to have the peace of God?

11. Have you ever fully experienced the peace of God?

12. What does joy and peace of God mean when we talk about perfect power?

13. How does God's power move in your life?

14. How does fear prevent you from having faith in God's protection?

15. Have you ever been paralyzed by fear? How did you react?

16. What does it mean to you when we say, "You can face all things through the peace that Christ has given you"?

---- C H A P T E R 3 ----

SESSION 4: YOU CAN'T JUDGE ME

If you judge people, you have no time to love them.
——Mother Teresa

Have you ever encountered someone who nitpicks everything? With reckless abandon, nitpickers criticize everything you do and how you do it, and they are always willing to give their expertise on any subject. When we encounter these people, we can easily feel judged, and their opinions pierce our lives to the absolute core. No matter how much we try to ignore them, we find ourselves being annoyed by their very presence because we know, when they come around, everything we do will be criticized and critiqued.

Churches are full of righteous nitpickers. In a defense of the gospel, they portray the enforcers of the sin passages in the Word, criticizing every sin listed but their own. Sometimes they will even tell other people how they might have struggled with a particular sin in their life and how they overcame it, but the reality is that true nitpickers will avoid their major sin issue. The reason they do this is to avoid accusation against something themselves.

I have witnessed righteous nitpickers in every church I have ever been in. These people believe they are defending the gospel but are really avoiding the responsibilities of their own sin. Using scripture as their backbone, they begin to tell everyone what is wrong with society. The instances where church members believe they are providing correction but are really retaliating for judging others happen almost every week. As a result, every week, people feel judged and rejected by the very people they came to find healing from. This isn't to say that there is a proper way to correct sin issues, but many times it will come across as judgment if it is not relayed properly.

There is another type of judge that many fail to look at. Those are the neighborhood gossips. They thrive on knowing everything that is going on in the neighborhood. When someone's child is home sick from school, they make sure to send out a text and social media post to warn everyone from going to that person's house until the child is better. The issues come into play when the gossip tells everyone about the argument he or she hears coming from someone's house or the disciplinary problem that people have with their children, and the list would go on.

It seems like gossips thrive on knowing what is happening in everyone's life. Even though some believe they are being a good "Christian" neighbor by warning the neighborhood of everyone's wrongdoing, many people will see them as a gossiping pest. I have encountered some gossips who make sure everyone knows they are good Christians. As they are about to gossip, they will start off by saying, "You know I'm a good Christian, and I shouldn't be telling you this, but I think we need to pray for …"

While they know it is not something that needs to be said, they use the excuse of asking for prayer as the reason to tell about everyone's issues in the neighborhood. Deep down inside, many of these gossips know they are wrong, but they also love a good juicy story about the neighbors.

When we encounter people who call into question our character, intent, or behaviors, we look at them as judgmental and overbearing. This does not open our minds to effective teaching and changes in behavior, but it puts us on defense. We look for ways to defend our actions and what we believe and even justify the outcome as good, even if it is not. When all else fails, we grab the best scripture we know about judgment and ensure people know that, before they judge us, they "must take the plank out of their own eye."

What we do not realize is how we overuse the statement. We have to understand the difference between biblical correction and placing judgment on others. When we are facing judgment, a very hurtful and damaging action can take away from the growth and development of the Christian church.

Emotionally, society uses the statement when they are hurt or upset over an issue. When someone comes to them and begins to correct them by pointing out something that needs to be changed, our defensiveness clouds our ability to rationalize with someone. Naturally we will either walk away embarrassed or engage in argument. By nature, people do not like to have their shortcomings pointed out to them.

Some people say they would rather have their shortcomings pointed out to them instead of looking bad in the eyes of other people, but in truth, it becomes bothersome and embarrassing. Simply put, people are hurt when they find out the things they thought were good and correct actually were not.

The emotional impact of using this statement can be devastating for people too. When someone thinks he or she is defending himself or herself and uses this statement, it causes believers who thought they were doing the right thing to question themselves. They wonder if they were placing judgment or if they should even try to correct others if the impact will be a personal attack on them.

The emotional and spiritual stressors from being attacked or accused can cause physiological impacts that affect personal health. Serious implications of stress-induced hypertension, heart disease, and other life-threatening illnesses can develop from stress. When these issues happen or begin to develop, it is best for the person to see his or her physician or seek professional help so he or she is able to recover from the impacts.

The spiritual impact weighs greater than any other characteristic in the holistic approach. All parties involved are damaged spiritually by the misuse of this statement. Those who are using the statement as a defense mechanism can become spiritually arrogant. Believing they are using it correctly, they gain a boldness to tell everyone the statement as the first line of defense against facing possible sinful behaviors. More so, they fail to face the "plank" or "speck" in their own eye because of their need to defend themselves.

Those who feel like they have been wrongfully accused of placing judgment begin to feel like they do not have a place to correct people because of their own issues. This creates apathy within the church and prevents people who should be corrected from proper teaching and reproof. This goes into the difference between judgment and correction, which is discussed further in this chapter.

Many people in church are getting away with sinful behaviors because they use scriptures in a way that prevents other people from challenging them. While they might know what they are doing, they take advantage of single-verse defense in hopes that no one challenges them.

Using a single-verse defense allows people to pull one verse from the Bible without looking at the context so they can defend or accuse people of things in a way that fits their preferred theologies or thought processes. This defense works especially well when people do not know where to look or how to research the verse in the Bible. By asking the person to show you the verse in the Bible, it helps to defuse the single-verse defense.

Looking at the Context

Those who use the statement, "take the plank out of your eye," are referring to Matthew 7:3–4. In this passage, Christ is teaching about people who are placing judgment on others. When just those two verses are read, it is easy to see where this passage can be used as a springboard defense against people who are judging and correcting.

Expanding the context of this passage to Matthew 7:1–6, we can learn a few lessons from Jesus's teaching. Understanding the meaning behind the log and specks will give us a better viewpoint of what happens when we judge others versus correcting them. Once we learn that judgment begets judgment, we can realize that Christ was talking about working on our own relationship with Christ before we begin to tell others how to fix their own spiritual lives.

Despite whether we are helping repair someone else's spiritual life, we also have to be gentle with the delicate balance between offering help and forcing help on others. Often we are so excited to help other people that we do not realize they might not be seeking our assistance. Having the wisdom and discernment to help when the Spirit moves is much like a doctor having the knowledge of treating a patient with the least invasive treatment plan possible.

Judgment Begets Judgment

People who use righteous judgment to correct people in the church generally think themselves to be men of great integrity. This is not because they are well-versed in the Bible. It's because they always try to do the right thing outside of their one little sin issue. Since they feel such high integrity, they take advantage of every opportunity to correct people when they think there is wrongdoing in the midst.

Making every attempt to hide their own personal issues, these people point out others' shortcomings. The issue was that they only point out the inadequacies of the things they do well, which caused the shortcoming to be overshadowed by their success. This will give them a feeling of control over their issue, and because they have control over issues they usually do not struggle with, they do not understand why others cannot control the issue.

Judging others can easily become a habit. Everyone a judger meets will place some level of judgment on someone. The people know it is a habit, and if it gets too bad, they will begin pointing out the shortcomings of a judger to help him or her understand how it feels. In positive outcomes, he or she soon realizes the people he or she spends most of his or her time with at home and work don't like him or her as much as he or she thinks.

Eventually a righteous judger will begin searching for direction from others. He or she desired something that would help him or her understand why people always found criticism with everything he or she does. After some digging, a helping agent can assist in figuring out how his or her dysfunctional past might have manifested itself in judgment of others as opposed to facing shortcomings. When these realizations are made, growth takes place, and the judger become less critical. The pride subsides to humility, which results in community.

Many of us are no different when it comes to picking out things we do not like about people. We have a need and desire to be accepted. If you grow up in a home where nothing was ever good enough, you could take one of two directions in the way you will manifest regressed emotions:

1. People will manifest their emotions by holding people to the same standard they were held to. This is a normal reaction based on the upbringing and normalized expectation in social development. When people grow up believing a certain standard is the appropriate standard, they will hold others to the same standard and believe those who do not hold the standard are dysfunctional. This opens the door for judgment based on personal standards.

2. On the other hand, people become so apathetic over issues that they fail to stand up for qualities and actions that are inappropriate in others. Those who know what it feels like to be corrected or disciplined for qualities that are less than perfect can shy away from holding any type of standard toward others at all. This comes in two forms:

   a. They believe they are not good enough to judge others. This is the "I've done so much wrong in my life, so what place do I have to judge someone else?" attitude.
   b. They know how it feels and do not want others to feel the same way. This sympathetic attitude avoids conflict based on avoidance.

Whether people are not afraid to shy away from placing judgment or they are very passive in order to avoid conflict, it is important for them to find the balance. They have to understand what Christ teaches in Matthew 7:1–6 regarding judgment and then make every attempt to understand and apply this teaching to their lives.

When Jesus was teaching the words, "Do not judge, so that you won't be judged" (Matt. 7:1), He was instructing people not to judge. Christ is teaching the people that judgment of others is also an open invitation for you to be judged. When we critically look at others with intolerance, the question has to be asked: Are we judging the person as a whole or just the unacceptable behaviors?

Often we are judging the person based on certain behaviors. When we take the time to learn more about him or her, we might find those behaviors are more quirks than intolerable habits. If they are not quirks or misperceptions, it is a behavior that should be corrected with care, not uncompassionate response to the situation.

Jesus simply says to not judge, but He furthers his statement in Matthew 7:2a when He tells the people, "For the judgment you use, you will be judged." If we are very judgmental of other people, we should also be prepared for judgment. This, however, is not judgment from others, but ultimate judgment.

It is easy to be critical of people who are not like us or do not enjoy the same things as we do. We might get away with being critical to other people, but in the eyes of God, we might not be getting away with as much as we think. God will hold us accountable for our treatment of others. If we are judging others based on what they have done in their lives just because we might struggle with the issue, we too will be judged equally before God.

In the second part of verse 2, Jesus makes this clear, "The measure you use, it will be measured to you." Intolerant judgmental behavior mixed with personal sin issues can bring a higher level of judgment on you. We all have to go before God some day and answer to our actions. If those actions were more inclined to criticize as opposed to correct, the measure and standard we will be held to will be equal, if not greater.

While it seems easy to exploit people for their sin issues or things they are doing wrong, we have to consider how we might be addressing the situation. By addressing others with a high level of love and respect, we might be able to nurture them toward a stronger relationship with Christ. The biggest thing we have to avoid is judgment of others as a coping mechanism to cover up our personal shortcomings.

REPAIRING YOURSELF BEFORE FIXING OTHERS

Doctors always fascinate me because some of them have an overwhelming amount of faith in God, while others see no need for the presence of God in their vocation. As a trauma chaplain, I have spent a great deal of time talking with trauma doctors about their belief in God or lack thereof. Some are agnostic, believing there is something out there, but they have a hard time figuring out who and how something greater than them interacts with them on a daily basis. I know several pediatric trauma doctors who struggle with this because they feel, if God existed, then why would he let the children face such traumatic events. (It's a good question, but not for this chapter.)

Many of them believe, when children come to the trauma bay, they have control and power to save the child's life. This is a good quality for a doctor because you definitely want to have a confident doctor working on your child. There is sometimes moral and spiritual conflict in the confidence of ability and God's ability.

I knew a doctor who was in the middle of a trauma procedure when he began having trouble with his peripheral vision. As soon as it started to happen, he stepped away from the procedure before any mistake might have been made. The doctor was frustrated because it was the first procedure he stepped away from in the many years he practiced trauma medicine.

Immediately the doctor went to the optometrist's office and found out that he had a small hole in his eye that would eventually render him blind if not corrected with surgery. The recovery would be long, and he would not be able to practice trauma medicine for nearly a year. Not only did the doctor have to walk away from the procedure that day, but he had to walk away from medicine for the time being.

I am certain as a parent myself that the parents of that child in the trauma bay would not want a blind doctor operating on their child, even if the doctor had full sight in one eye and was only partially blind. Just as the doctor walked away from that child, sometimes we have to walk away from correcting others because of the sinful behaviors present in our own lives.

We cannot have double vision. With one eye, we can see the Christian standards clearly, and with the other eye, we blur them for our own benefit. If you think about it, this is a common practice in our world today. It takes the roll of "Do as I say, not as I do." Holding a double standard serves as a self-gratifying action that will destroy relationships.

We have a tendency to attack people with half the vision we should because our own sin issues render us partially blind. This is the meat of what Jesus was telling the people in the following verses of Matthew 7:3–5. In these three verses, it is interesting that Christ says the same thing in three different ways. First, He asks the question. Then He makes the statement in the form of the question and gives the solution in a direct and concise way.

Jesus asks a question we should be asking ourselves when we would like to speak with people about an issue (Matt. 7:3). Why do we look at the speck in other people's eyes but do not notice the log in our own eye? This question challenges us beyond our normal bias. If we believe we do the right thing all the time, we become biased to the way we believe it should be done. This thought process develops two reactions that impact approaching someone regarding his or her issue.

First, we have to understand that finding fault with others is easier because, when we are forced to look into our own lives, things we do not like about ourselves are revealed. For example, if I were pessimistic about every situation I enter and there is someone who is overly optimistic, it would be easy to say their heads are in the clouds all the time and they do not have a good grasp on reality. In actuality they might be gifted in looking at situations with the ideals to overcome, whereas my thinking is, "What might happen if the idea does not work, so why even try?" There might be a happy medium, but in both cases, there is healthy judgment that can take place if it impacts God's calling in someone's life.

God places people of different values and viewpoints in each other's lives so we can achieve a common goal. When that goal is not able to be achieved because our judgment of the other person gets in the way of capitalizing on their gifting, we get in the way of God. When we go before divine judgment, we have to answer as to why we impeded the Holy Spirit from moving in a situation because our opinions of other people prevented us from working with them.

The key to situations is to look at people in an optimistic way. Instead of our judgment based in opinion getting in the way, we can allow positive influence into our lives by asking why God might have placed someone in our lives and for what purpose.

As hard as it might be to work with someone, the purpose God has put us together is so that we might sharpen one another in the midst of our own weakness. While he or she might have a major sin issue you can help him or her overcome, opening your life to him or her and being vulnerable might help you get past the hurdle of your sin issue.

Some trauma doctors blame God for the traumas they face every day, but in reality, many have a hard time believing humanity would be so careless with human life once you really talk with them. Instead of praising God for giving the skills to help in the repair process of those who come in their trauma bay and encouraging parents, they chose to shoulder the responsibility of life and death on their own. When the doctor mentioned above faced the incident with his eye, he had been so successful for so many years that he did not know where to turn when his pride of control had to be surrendered to someone else.

The second reason we do not realize our vision is impaired when it comes to judgment is adaptation to the issue. Having an issue in your life so long that it has become part of you can be hazardous to coping with other people. When we adapt to sin issues in our lives, they become natural actions and reactions despite what others might tell us.

Despite the sin issue having a part of your life so that it becomes part of you, it is an adopted part of your personality, actions, and character. I have a pinched sciatic nerve in my back. When I first developed the issue, it was very painful, and I was afraid to move certain ways or do certain things. As I progressed with the issue, seeing a spinal orthopedist helped alleviate the pain, but I still have the issue. The difference is that I have dealt with it for so long that I no longer walk hunched over or remain sensitive to the pain. I have adapted to the pain and continue with my daily activities. Only when it becomes agitated after doing an extra hard workout do I have issues and realize it is there.

When we place judgment on other people, we are not even thinking about our personal issue because it is not changing the way we live our lives. If I were to hold a group counseling session where I told everyone to share his or her most secret sin that he or she is not able to overcome, besides being very damaging emotionally, this group would most likely start out with judgment but end with a great deal of understanding. When we realize that people have sin in different ways but all are imperfect, we realize there is not a lot of room to judge those who sin differently from us.

This is the point that Jesus makes when he stands before the crowd and tells those without sin to cast the first stone at the adulteress woman (John 8:2–11). It is important to point out that those who were testing Him were considered the Jewish religious leaders. The leaders who were empowered to enforce the law were not able to cast a stone because they too had sinned against God. This sin forced the Pharisees to walk away from Jesus and the adulteress woman, rendering their judgment of her invalid.

Some Christians believe it is their job to call out people on various sin issues. When they get the opportunity to place judgment on whether they are qualified to get to heaven or if they have a true relationship with Christ, they jump on the chance. If the person does not reply the way those placing judgment on him or her think he or she should, then they begin to spread the judgment. These people are so blind to their own sin issues that they do not realize the importance of stepping back and changing their own lives before trying to change others.

When the trauma doctor realized that something was not right, he stepped away from the procedure. This might have been the precursor to God bringing him back to faith, but the reality was that, just like a sin issue in our lives, he was used to being able to perform routine procedures with ease. When his eyesight became impaired, he stopped trying to repair the person on the table and began attempting to correct his own issue.

As hurtful as it was, he knew he could not assist the person in the trauma bay that day because he needed help himself. This realization could have been disastrous if he would have continued. The damage he might have caused to the person receiving the procedure could have been irreversible because he would have made maneuvers despite his impairment. By him walking away, someone else, who was not blinded, was able to step in and restore the patient.

When we have issues in our lives, we have to be able to walk away and fix those issues before we can try to help others in their situations. This is the point that Christ is making in verse 4. How are we able to fix the issue in someone else's life when we might be operating with one eye? We have to be able to see clear from both eyes to assist in delicately extracting sin from someone else.

When I say "assist in delicately extracting sin," we have to understand that it is not up to us to remove sin from people, but the conviction of the Holy Spirit. If we believe that our judgment and criticism will get them to turn from sinful behaviors, we, once again, are operating with impaired vision. The Holy Spirit convicts. Only He can prompt someone to seek forgiveness, and only God can give eternal forgiveness. Submitting the control and power of judgment, conviction, and forgiveness to the Holy Spirit will allow us the freedom to love the person unconditionally.

Just as the Holy Spirit provides conviction and forgiveness, it is our job to come alongside the person and walk the difficult path of healing with him or her. We can't just condemn him or her and walk away. We gently help identify the issue and seek his or her permission to walk alongside that individual. In some cases, we can only identify the issue and allow the Holy Spirit to do the rest. This is why it is important to prayerfully address an issue before openly addressing it. When we have prayed over an issue, we are able to focus on an unconditional love that supersedes all transgressions. Those who are facing sin issues need to experience care, compassion, and support before they experience condemnation if we truly want to see them submit to the Holy Spirit.

This unconditional love will allow us to see past the sin issue and directly at the person. If we are not able to look at who the person is in the eyes of God, we are not able to submit to our own self-righteous behaviors that impair our ability to grow spiritually. We have to be able to step back and work on removing the log in our own eyes because our inability to see clearly inhibits our relationship, not other people.

This is why Jesus used the drastic difference between the two items. First, a splinter or speck is small and can cause irritation or blurred vision, but it can also be flushed out with some water. On the other hand, a log is blinding and more difficult to remove, and it takes a lot of work to repair. Christ is telling the people they have a lot of work to do on themselves, and without doing that effort, they will not be able to see clear enough to even flush out a speck from their brother's eyes.

What we might believe is a log in another person's life might only be a speck in their spiritual lives. Placing judgment on the speck once again fails to pay attention to how healthy the rest of the body might be. If we have enough sin in our lives to blind us, we should begin removing that sin so we might be spiritually healthy too.

Removing the sin from our eyes begins with seeking the Holy Spirit. Asking that our sin is revealed to us so we can have a deeper relationship with God is the first step in removing the log from our eyes. Second, once the sin is revealed to us, we have to ask God for forgiveness. The third step is the difference between asking forgiveness and seeking repentance. You have to make an intentional change that eradicates that sin from your life. Once the sin is removed, you have to be constantly on guard that it does not come back.

We have to remember that God does forgive all sin. However, whenever Jesus forgave sin, He always told the person, "Go, and sin no more." If we are to honestly remove the log from our eyes, we have to follow through with the final statement. You have to make a life change that makes every attempt to prevent the log from being lodged in your eye once again. This attempt does not mean you will never get a speck or splinter, but it does mean you will prevent the spiritual impairment of permanent sin in your life.

Jesus is passionate in verse 5 when He calls sinful broken people hypocrites for trying to repair other people even though they themselves are broken. Specifically, he is telling the people they have to fix themselves before they can try to fix other people. If we are not able to work on our own sin issues, there is no possible way we are able to see clear enough to help correct other people. We will look at the difference between correction and judgment in the next section of this chapter. The key is to see clear before we engage other people. A clear sight picture allows the Holy Spirit to move through you without trying to hurdle the sin issues in your life that prevent pure intentions.

If the trauma doctor would have continued the procedure and something happened, he would have most likely been sued for malpractice. Doctors have to be so careful on every move they make to ensure they are making the right action. If they are not able to address the issue, they have to call in a specialist. When the trauma doctor had the issue with his sight, he could no longer take care of his personal health by himself. He had to call in a specialist to help him out. He knew he was not qualified to repair his eye.

When we know there are issues that must be addressed in our lives and continue placing judgment on others, we are committing malpractice of the Christian faith. If we are not able to disciple someone because we are struggling with the same issue that we have not yet begun to overcome, we have to find someone else to guide them. We should always be looking for people who can pour wisdom into our lives without judgment. These people can be those who have faced the same sin and overcame, or they can be people who have never struggled with the sin. No matter what level they are, they cannot be people who are struggling at the same level as us.

In order to avoid Christian malpractice, we have to avoid judgment and know when to step away from someone. This wisdom comes from being open to the divine intervention of the Holy Spirit. Without Him, we are impaired, we will not be able to remove sin from our lives, and we will never be able to see clear enough to assist in guiding others to salvation and redemption in Jesus Christ.

DON'T PUSH RELIGION ON THOSE WHO DON'T WANT IT

Have you ever walked through a department store and been ambushed by a perfume model spraying everyone walking by? There was a time they would spray you and not even ask. If you were in their zone, you were an open target to walk through their mist of perfume.

Over time, the rules have changed though. If you see a perfume model in a department store nowadays, he or she will ask if you would like to try the newest scent from the line he or she is representing. If you say no, he or she will move on to the next person. If you say yes, he or she will spray a small piece of cardboard and hand it to you. Should you like the smell, you can ask the model to spray it on you as a sample.

I am sure these rules changed because big, burly guys trying to get through the department store were sick of spending the rest of the day smelling like spring flowers after walking through an odorous mist of eau de toilette. I am sure the frustration after being hijacked by the perfume models was bothersome and annoying, especially if they were not even shopping for perfume, let alone desiring to try some.

When we learn about the above passage on judgment, we love to use the first five verses as a defensive measure, but we rarely hear them talking about verse 6. Jesus gives a warning to people who are chronic correctors through an if-then scenario that will help us understand that not everyone cares about what we might have to say.

When we judge people, even in the name of making their lives better, sometimes people just do not want to hear it. This happens because people are not prepared to change, do not want to change, or are satisfied with their lives the way they are. Each of these devices is blinding, and it is up to the Holy Spirit to restore their sight. We have to be available as a tool of the Holy Spirit, but we cannot try to be the Assistant Holy Spirit by speaking on His behalf when we have not been called to do so.

Volunteering correction or judgment and having people accept it requires a discernment and openness to the Holy Spirit's prompting. As well, we have to determine if our criticism is constructive or destructive in nature. In the first part of verse 6, Jesus tells the people, "Don't give what is holy to dogs, or toss your pearls before pigs."

When He is talking about dogs, Jesus was not referring to the domesticated dog that you might play fetch with. He was talking about wild animals that do not hold value in the things that are given to them. These dogs can be translated into the people who are offered words of advice or wisdom, and they will only take from it what they believe might benefit them. They can never be domesticated because they will never leave their pack. The people they hold company with most often will always influence their decisions.

Do not take your most treasured understanding of the faith and toss it to someone who will ravish it and disappear, only to come back later when that person cannot find what he or she is looking for on his or her own or from the world. Once this happens, not only will you feel used and abused, but you will also become frustrated.

Have you ever given so much time to someone, only to be ignored? I know when I pour out my effort to help someone, only to be ignored in the end, I become frustrated and used. This happens because I am casting the seed in the wrong places (Luke 8:4–8). God has already prepared the ground for the harvest, and we have to be in the right place and know how to plant and grow the seed in order to reap the harvest. Throwing what is holy to the dogs is like wasting the seeds of wisdom by throwing it on the path and stony areas, only to be trampled, eaten, or withered away.

The second part of this example is tossing pearls to pigs. Wisdom is a valuable thing, and not everyone understands or respects experience and wisdom. Today's culture qualifies people based on action and proof, not experience and qualifications. There is a thought that college degrees, time, and experience might be good for old war stories because society has made it so easy to obtain education and experience, but to the younger generation, it is not good for corporate advancement. In this part of the statement, Christ is saying, "Do not give the best of what you have to people who are not going to listen because they have never taken heed to past experience."

Even though these people might desperately need a change in their lives, they do not want to put the effort into making the change. Sometimes we have to accept that people who do not want to change will not adapt unless their own circumstances force them. This is especially true if the person you are providing correction to continually replies with "That's what everyone tells me." I always follow the adage that people will change when the pain of staying the same is greater than the pain of changing.

Some people feel beaten and battered by the simple address of judgment and become aggressive in an attempt to defend their position. Jesus makes the point that we should not force these things on others, because if we do, "they will trample them with their feet, turn, and tear you to pieces" (Matt. 7:6b). The one word that stands out here is "will." Christ does not say they might trample you. He says they *will* trample you. This gives us the direct warning that if we tell people things they are not ready to hear, there is no doubt that we will be retaliated against.

This is important when telling people about sin issues as well as behaviors that are inappropriate as a Christian. Even more, it brings to light the discernment that has to take place when sharing the gospel message with other people.

Sometimes Christians are excited to point out sin and not as eager to love the sinner despite the sin. Building a trust relationship that opens the doors for other people is important. Simply demanding repentance without a relationship is like being an out-of-control perfume model that sprays everyone with his or her product because this individual believes people are not attractive and stink without it.

Perfume models have changed their tactics because their approach was aggressive and uninviting. They attempt to build momentary relationship with people. By giving people an opportunity to smell the scent and allowing the scent to speak for itself in a nonthreatening way, a patron's defense mechanisms are lowered. Then when the person is ready and has decided at his or her own free will, the consumer allows the scent to be sprayed on him or her.

As Christians, we have to be wise when pointing out issues with other people. We have to build the relationship with them. Give opportunity for them to experience the Holy Spirit for themselves. When the time is right and the Holy Spirit has prepared their hearts, they will immerse themselves in the blessed gift of salvation.

Jesus makes a valid statement in this passage, which, used in the right context, prompts life-changing principles. Christ is talking about the people who are placing judgment on others but living sinful lifestyles themselves. First, He makes the point that we have no place to judge someone for what he or she might be doing because we might be dealing with something far worse.

We have to remove the sin from our lives before we can begin trying to correct someone for the sin issues in his or her life. By evaluating the passage, it can be debated as to the appropriateness of statements such as

"You can't judge me" or "Only God is my judge." According to Christ, they are correct, but we cannot use this as a defense mechanism when people are trying to better our lives, spiritually or personally. Judgment is acceptable, but be prepared to be judged at the same harshness in which you have placed judgment.

Finally we have to be wise about who we are supposed to approach to provide correction. While we might be called to critically judge people, we are called to hold each other accountable in a way that will restore them in the faith (Gal. 6:1–2) and inspire them toward love and good things by building each other up in Christ (Heb. 10:24; 1 Thess. 5:11).

What We Should Use Instead

In harmony, we realize that Christ was teaching Matthew 7:1–6 not as a defensive statement used to shut people up but to let them know how important it is for them to build people up. We do not hold people to our objective standards, but we must hold them to Christian standards that are universal across all denominations. Biblical insight and understanding as well as being able to show people in the Bible where the point of correction comes from can only back this standard. Knowing the Christian standard allows us to avoid judgment and form our thoughts and actions toward correction when we see a Christian brother or sister doing something wrong.

A delicate balance allows people to understand if they are judging the person for what he or she does or correcting him or her to be a better disciple. People should ask themselves four questions to determine if they are providing correction or placing judgment on someone. When people ask themselves these questions, a considerable amount of time should be taken to ensure their intentions, position, and attitude are in the right place before engaging the other person.

Sometimes the intentions for helping others are in the right place. We become empathetic to their needs and honestly care about their spiritual development but fall short because our attitudes do not reflect the care and concern we want to give in the situation.

Attitude is very important because the way we approach people contributes to how they will receive the message. If we communicate our needs or desires to someone with an abrupt attitude and he or she prefers a more gentle approach, he or she will not receive the message. On the other hand, if he or she prefers the blunt, abrupt approach, he or she would not receive a gentle message of change.

For the person who is trying to communicate a need for change, he or she has to know whom he or she is talking to and ensure his or her approach matches the recipient's ability to receive the message. This becomes the difference between self-satisfying behavior and honest desire to help other people. If we are willing to bypass our own personal desire in order to help other people, we will make every attempt to learn how the recipient will receive our message. On the other hand, if we are not willing to learn this aspect of positive communication, we are fulfilling our own desires of getting annoyances off our chests.

Talking to people about our frustrations with them in a way that does not consider their feelings or need for compassion does not attempt to change the other person. This behavior only attempts to change our feelings of frustration by getting the emotional weight off our chests and transferring it to the other person. While this might institute change in his or her life for a short time, often the person will revert to inappropriate behaviors because the only message he or she received was frustration, not true care for the person's renewed behavior.

AUTHORITY

One of the first ways you can determine if you are judging or correcting someone is by evaluating your authority or permission to speak into his or her life. People who are satisfied in their behavior or activities rarely accept involuntary criticism or mentorship. If we place our effort in ensuring their behaviors are corrected, we will naturally be rejected because we do not have permission to speak into their lives.

We have to continually pray for discernment so we know when we should speak into someone's life. Without discernment, we will not know when we are forcing our thoughts on someone or if they will be openly received. Even when we ask permission to give others advice, we have to be cautious about how we advise them as well as what we counsel them about.

Various boundaries are set up in people's lives, and once those boundaries are crossed, it is easy to become defensive. This is all based in the authority we have to speak into people's lives. Each person has a hierarchy of authority figures. People place the importance of opinion based on their trust and respect for people in their lives.

My boss has more authority to speak into my life than a subordinate does. Therefore if a subordinate asks me to do something to help him or her and it directly conflicts with direction from my boss, not only does that create a moral issue, but I would have to follow my boss's direction first. In this example, my boss holds the higher level of authority than the subordinate does.

When it comes to providing correction for people, we have to know the trust and respect level the other person has for us. Simply remember it takes longer to gain someone's respect than it does to lose it. If we cross the boundary of authority to speak into someone's life, it could easily ruin our chances of gaining his or her respect and opportunity to correct this person's actions through love.

Our level of authority to speak into someone's life also comes from knowing where God has called us to serve others. We have to understand that we are God's creation, and through that creation, we are designed to do good works that God prepared for us to walk in (Eph. 2:10). This means that if God has called us to do something, we will walk in the goodness of God.

God gives us the call and authority to address issues with people. Our calling is based in how God has gifted us through the Holy Spirit. Every Christian has the same basic call, which is to make disciples and then baptize and teach them to observe what Christ has commanded (Matt. 28:18–19). The variations of that call is to do what God has called you to do within the boundaries of how people let you answer that call.

If someone is a medical doctor, he or she has to correct people based on his or her medical knowledge. This knowledge allows him or her to speak with authority to his or her patients, while he or she might think something is a sin issue, the doctor would tell the person of its damaging health effects before he or she would say it was sinful. This does not make him or her any less of a Christian, but it displays the ways God will reveal issues in someone's life in a way he or she might receive it.

In the same manner, someone who sees his or her friend engaging in addictive behaviors that can damage his or her health and well-being might not be able to talk about the medical issues as much as he or she can speak to the social damage it might be causing in the friendship. These boundaries allow people to speak with authority in others' lives in a way that the issue might be received.

Where we go wrong is when we believe we have the right to speak into people's lives outside where we are called to do so. When I was working in ministry, I was sitting with a family that just got bad news about the impending death of a loved one. As the doctor gave the family their news, the social worker asked me to say a few words of encouragement.

"I can't imagine what your feeling right now," I told the family.

As they sat in silence I continued, " It might take some time to process your feelings, but I am available to help answer the difficult spiritual questions you might have, when they are ready."

When I was finished, the doctor said something to the effect that, since I wouldn't give them comfort as the pastor, she would offer comfort herself. The doctor then began to give them canned words of meaningless encouragement that was visibly upsetting everyone in the room. When she finally stopped talking, one family member said thanks and politely ushered the doctor out of the room, asking me to stay and talk.

In this case, the doctor wanted to correct their emotional response to the news that she felt was bad in a time where solid decisions needed to be made. On the other hand, I let the family be in the moment with the emotions they had so they could process the information, ask appropriate questions, and make informed decisions, spiritually, emotionally, and physically.

The doctor did not have the authority to speak about spiritual issues to this family in this manner and ended up ruining the family's trust level in their loved one's care. The doctor was making a judgment call on what she felt the family needed and did not understand the spiritual dynamics of the family's situation.

We have to understand that, without proper permission or authority, we are most likely placing judgment on them and not providing correction. Use these points to ensure you have the right authority to provide corrections:

- Know where you stand.
- Ask permission.

- Speak within your calling.
- Never degrade them.
- Talk about the effects of the behavior.

If these five points are taken into consideration, you will have a clear understanding regarding your authority to speak into the life of someone when he or she is engaging in a biblically sinful behavior.

ATTITUDE

I have written it many times in this chapter, but it is easy to find things we do not like about someone. Each person we meet will always present reasons why he or she should not be liked or why it would be difficult to love him or her as a human being. If you want to provide mentorship and correction to someone, you have to be willing to love your neighbor, even when he or she makes it difficult to be loved.

This is the point that Jesus was trying to relay as he was teaching about loving God and loving your neighbor (Mark 12:29–32). Six aspects to loving your neighbor will help you know if you are judging people or trying to help them through mentorship and correction.

Of the six, only two of them are "you" statements, while the remaining four are "them" statements. "You" statements are things that are designed to institute change in yourself. These changes require personal self-evaluation and a solid plan to modify your own behavior. "Them" statements are not things they have a part in changing, but things you must do to them in order to develop a relationship that allows for the open flow of mentorship.

The first step to loving your neighbor is to be who God made you to be. So often we put on a mask of who we are for people around us. This mask is what we think people want us to be, but might not always be who we actually are. When we pretend to be someone else, our desire to be a better person than we actually are gets in the way of grace for the imperfections of other people.

We have to be careful because, if the person we are is not someone that we should be, that would bring us back to the Matthew 7 passage listed above. If we are judgmental, mean, and critical of everyone, we need to do some work on ourselves to be who God created us to be. With the ability to identify ourselves as children of God with the best intentions for others, we can no longer lie to ourselves and have to come to terms with who we are before we can begin a change in ourselves. It is impossible to love our neighbors if we have failed to love who we are as well.

When we try to be someone else, we make the mistake of letting our personal desires to receive righteous recognition get in the way of our desires to disciple other people. The second action needed to love our neighbors is sacrificing our personal desires and see beyond what we want and look toward what might be better for the other person. There is something inherent in us that desires to be liked. Even if the person does not like us or we do not like the other person, we want to be liked by him or her and will do anything to have him or her like us. Sometimes trying too hard to be liked by someone will distort our ability to see that we do not have to be liked by everyone, and we do not have to like everyone either. The fact is that we have to love him or her for who he or she is if Christ is in us, and we want to show who Christ is in our lives.

This is the most difficult aspect of loving our neighbors because we like people who are like us. When I listen to people who are dating, it is always interesting to hear the person's idea of the perfect match for him or her. I knew one person who did not like the side of the head her boyfriend parted his hair on, so she attempted to change that part of him. Her desire was to change the side of the hair he parted for many reasons, none of which was acceptance of who he was when they met. Her thought was she would start with something easy and ease into the more difficult things she did not like about him as the relationship got more serious.

Just as the woman tried to change her boyfriend into what she wanted or thought the model man should be, as Christians, we sometimes place such heavy judgment on people to change them into the model Christian for our purpose and means. When this happens, we fail to recognize who God molded them to be in His greater picture in life. Small quirks that are not part of unbiblical sin should not be nitpicked by brothers in sisters in Christ, but prayerfully considered for their place in the greater purpose of the kingdom.

The fact is, if we negatively approach those we want to mentor or disciple, we will never be satisfied with who they are. Our dissatisfaction with other people can sometimes be a desire to make them someone we will like better. Our job is not to make someone we will like better; our duty as Christians is to help him or her understand the damage he or she might be causing to himself or herself and others through sinful behavior. Sacrificing our own desires means that sometimes we just have to walk away from the issue or learn to love him or her for who he or she is, depending on the status of your relationship.

We have to understand that our opinion of people is based on what we see. We see the person for how he or she looks, the way he or she acts, or how he or she relays messages. When we do that, we have to remember he or she is also having a struggle within himself or herself, especially if he or she is struggling with a sin issue he or she cannot overcome. Only God can see the true heart of the person (1 Sam. 16:7), and because He is the only person who sees everyone's heart and desires, our job is to focus on loving him or her despite our personal desires to help him or her change.

Making self-corrections will allow us to help the other person with the right heart. As aforementioned, we cannot help other people if we are dysfunctional ourselves. When we know that our authority and self-development allow us to address issues with other people in our lives, we first need to seek them out. When we seek out our neighbor, it does not mean we constantly search for people to help.

Have you ever met someone that always talked about the people he or she helped? It always seems like he or she is so busy helping someone overcome some trial or situation in others' lives that he or she can't comprehend the issues of his or her own life. As a compliment, I told some I encounter that it is such a blessing that God is bringing all these people into his or her life. Often he or she will reply that sometimes it had become a burden, but the feeling he or she got from helping people makes him or her feel really good.

As the conversations with chronic helpers progress, I realize that assisting other people is like a drug to them. If they don't have someone to help through a difficult time in life, many of them search for people to assist and sometimes create a crisis so they are able to fix it for them. Soon I realized that chronic helpers are addicted to helping people and can't stop helping them because of the high they get by knowing they had successfully overcome their issue with the chronic helpers assistance.

When I say we have to seek our neighbor, this is not what I mean by seeking our neighbor. We do not have to look far for people to love on. Everyone needs some level of love, and if he or she has invited you into his or her life, you have the opportunity to show him or her love.

There has been a social shift in modern culture. When I was growing up, everyone knew each other in the neighborhood. My parents watched the neighbor's children, and the neighbors watched us. We had community picnics, and we genuinely cared about each other. Nowadays it seems as if knowing the person who lives next door to you might result in a burden. Having close friends means people who are emotionally close to you, and that is even considered a special relationship.

When we seek out our neighbor, it might be as easy as knowing who the person next door to you is or might require getting to know the person who works in the office down the hall is. It is not having relationships that equates to acquaintances, but relationships that allow you to know the burdens and struggles of the people in your life.

When I refer to seeking your neighbor, it is an action of getting to know people beyond what you think will keep him or her at just enough distance that he or she will not know who you are as well. We like to know about other people but think about how we keep ourselves guarded in the process.

Relationships are about give-and-take. We do not have to give all our dirt in life, but in the same respect, we can't expect everyone else to give us all the dirt in his or her life. When we have sought out people with a level of care and compassion that allows us to know who they really are, we too can open up our lives to them. This is the foundation of intimate friendships. They do not have to be your bestie, but he or she can be a confidante.

The second "they" way you can change your heart attitude toward someone is to bless him or her. As you get to know people, you learn what stressors they have in their lives. We have the unique ability to provide blessings to people when they least expect it through simple acts or actions. Even if you do not like the person, when your goal is to bless the person, you might be able to change his or her attitude and your heart toward the relationship.

Paul writes in the book of Romans that we should bless those who persecute us and we should not curse them (Rom. 12:14). When we bless those who persecute us, it shows that we are better able to see beyond the uncomfortable situation for the future hope of relationship. As I look back, some of the strongest relationships I have are those where conflict was present in the beginning or shortly after I had met the person. This was because both of us were willing to work out our differences and find a way to respect each other despite viewpoints or actions.

The more we had gotten to know each other, the more we realized we had similar viewpoints spiritually and morally that allowed us to see past the personality differences. When we face people who are not able to get past the personality differences, it is best that we do not force our blessing on them, but this does not mean that we do not continue to pray for them (Matt. 5:44). Our prayers carry more weight than any blessing we try to force on someone might carry.

I worked a job where it seemed like my coworker would find some reason to criticize me in everything I did. Eventually the relationship was so strained that I began to reciprocate the same feelings. Eventually it got so bad that we began physically fighting in the workplace.

When we walked away from each other, it seemed to me that nothing would ever change, and I just wanted to quit the job and walk away from it all. While I began to look for another job, I also began praying for the individual. Every day I would ask God to change his heart, but more for God to remove the bitterness from my heart.

This went on for a few weeks. The two of us could not even look at each other. I was not seeking him out, and I really was not trying to make a change in my own life. I was using prayer as an excuse to say I was being the better man. Then my coworker I was fighting with had a devastating accident in his life where he lost a loved one. I went to his house and sat with his family for a few hours, and then after some personal struggle, I offered to officiate the funeral for his family at no cost. I knew he did not have a lot of money, and this would take some of the expense off the burial costs.

That was a pivotal moment in our relationship as he accepted. I knew he was leery about my offer because he told another coworker I must be up to something to help him out the way I did, and he was just waiting for me to "cash in the favor." Years have gone by, and I no longer work that job or have contact with the previous coworker, but I never asked him for a favor nor brought up what I did for his family.

When we seek to bless the person, God will give us the opportunity when the timing is right. When we show that our attitude is not one of destruction and damage to other people, we have the opportunity to show love through blessing despite what the other person might think we are trying to do. Blessing someone is not about giving without the expectation of something in return, but also not bringing up the blessing as a reminder or holding over someone's head, waiting for the perfect moment to cash in a favor.

The third aspect to changing your attitude from judgment to correction is to listen to his or her story. Everyone has a story to tell. If we do not know his or her story, we will never know who he or she is as a person. Learn to understand where people have been and what they have done in life. Our understanding can mitigate so many misperceptions about people—who they are and what makes them act the way they do.

It is easy for us to get angry with people because of our differences. When we get angry, we capitalize on their shortcomings. Think about the last time you got angry with someone and why you were angry with him or her. I am willing to bet you were not angry because he or she was a good musician or had an excellent head of hair. It was because he or she did something that conflicted with what you wanted or expected from him or her. Instead of hearing his or her reasoning for the issue, you allowed your emotion in the situation to manifest into anger.

James writes in the Bible that we should be quick to hear and slow to speak and slow to anger because anger does not accomplish the righteousness of God (James 1:19). In my story above, I conflicted with the personality of the other guy. We were constantly angry at each other. Neither of us took the time to listen to each other's story. If I would have taken the time to hear his story, I would have understood he was taking care of an ailing loved one.

When we listen to people, we are not only listening to what they are saying verbally but also listening to what they are not saying. People will speak louder with their attitudes and actions than they will with their words. It is often hard to articulate in words what we might be feeling. Our society has created an environment that does not allow us to do so unless you are going through therapy. However, it is beyond our control when we communicate without words. We do not have to know what is going on to know something is wrong with someone.

If we think there might be something wrong with someone, we have the opportunity to ask him or her if everything is okay. It is his or her choice to share the issue with us or not, but no matter, we have to respect him or her in that decision. Respect is the final "them" statement when it comes to loving your neighbor.

I have seen many people get upset because they knew something was wrong with someone and continued to push the person into telling them what the issue was. Sometimes the greatest form of having a loving attitude toward someone is to respect his or her decision not to share an issue with you.

Sometimes this take a great deal of discernment. Colossians 4:8 instructs us to pray that doors will be open for us to share the message. Even more, we should act wise toward others and make the most of our time. Finally we should speak with grace so we may know how to answer people. If we are going to point out shortcomings in people's lives, we have to be able to speak with a level of grace that displays the love of Christ in our lives.

When we place judgment on people, we can speak without understanding. We are well intentioned, and we do not know what they might be dealing with personally to make them act in a way that does not show love. Sometimes it can be sin issues in their lives, and all we can do is pray that God convicts them or puts someone in their life that has the authority to speak. Sometimes they might be dealing with a difficult issue in their life, and it is so overwhelming they do not know whom they can talk to about it. Regardless of the issue, we have to be prayerfully ready to understand them and seek to love them despite how much they frustrate us.

If they have frustrated you beyond seeing any good in them, you are most likely correcting the person out of anger, malice, or hate. This does not seek to improve their life, but destroy their confidence. If you are able to capitalize on their strengths in order to overcome their weakness, you will naturally gravitate toward correction, not judgment.

Personality

Personality conflicts are hard to overcome and contribute the greatest amount of criticism for people. When we do not like someone's personality for whatever reason, we begin to find fault with everything about him or her. Even things that are perfectly acceptable become intolerable issues. It is a natural response to an emotion. This leads to inexcusable judgment of every action or word spoken. Our perception based on what he or she might have or have not done to us becomes a point of excuse for greater disagreement.

There is a story I have heard from many people about a man who had a personality conflict with someone else in the church. This man was one of the deacons and taught Sunday school. The other man he did not like was also a Sunday school teacher and sung in the choir. The deacon did not sing in the choir because the other man was in the choir; the choir member was not a deacon because the other man was a deacon.

The two had such great personality conflicts that each criticized the other's ministry in the church. "Would you listen to how that man sings? So out of key." Even though there was nothing wrong with his singing.

"If I were a deacon, I would make sure all my people were taken care of," the other said, even though there was nothing wrong with the way he was serving others.

The issue was creating such a great divide that the pastor had to sit the two down and talk with them about their issue. They were placing judgment on each other based on personal opinion, not biblical standards. This kind of judgment has plagued our Christian communities today, and it's very damaging to the church. We find reason to criticize the young people, the music, pastor, or any other person we feel might not fit our particular needs. When this happens, we have to understand that personality plays the biggest role in Satan's plan to destroy the church. In order to determine if personality is getting in the way of our opportunity to mentor someone, we can use two simple methods.

If we are using the Bible to provide correction, we are able to guide people biblically, not personal preference. We have to be careful, though, because it is too easy for us to use the Bible as our backing but not use it correct. That is the entire purpose behind this book. Using the Bible in the right context to back our correction of people is what the introductory session describes. When we are not using the Bible to correct someone, we are allowing our personalities to get in the way of ministering to the other person.

We often place judgment on people based on what we believe should be the right or wrong things for their lives. There are times when things are obviously wrong to do, but people believe there is nothing wrong with their particular behavior because they do not recognize what it is doing to others around them. When this happens, we have to ask ourselves if there is a cultural or personal issue with them or if the behavior is socially viewed as inappropriate.

Even when we use the Bible, we have to be careful of cultural or social differences. These differences—along with life experiences—mature us and give us an understanding of what the Bible says. We cannot expect everyone to be on the same level of understanding that we are biblically. We also cannot expect people who are not on the same level biblically to do the right things even if they have a greater amount of knowledge. Everyone has sin in his or her life, and when we have sin in our lives and a great deal of biblical knowledge, we can fool ourselves into finding loopholes in the scriptures.

There are people with biblical degrees at all levels who have grievous sin issues in their lives. When they are called on the sin issues, they often respond with matters of grace and mercy from God. Even more, they manipulate the Bible to reach their ultimate goal of not getting rid of the sin issue, but removing the sin accusation. They will use verses out of context and even justify why the person has the right to live his or her life.

These people use the Bible to get what they want while the accuser uses the Bible as a means to correct the behavior. As they work through the issues, often those wiser in the Word use their knowledge as a strong suit to argue their point, ultimately intimidating the other person to the point they give up and have a misunderstanding of the Word themselves. Because the accuser might not as academically astute as the other, the scholar undermines the guidance of the Holy Spirit.

These people use their knowledge of the Bible to demean others and cause them to call into question their ability to correct others. In these cases, the misuser's manipulation overpowers their correct use of the scriptures. When we are using scripture, it is important that we use them with the intention of edification, not the desire to win battles because we know them better than the other person does.

The other issue we might come into when we try to correct people using the scriptures is their rejection of biblical correction. All too often I have seen couples that get into an argument, and when the Bible is used to provide correction, one or the other begins to feel convicted and tells his or her spouse that he or she doesn't need to hear righteous preaching.

Using the Bible to provide correction for people will bring on conviction that is difficult to argue. The natural defense for most people is to reject them and claim it as the other person getting religious or preachy with them. This defense mechanism is a method we use to avoid the conviction caused by truth found in the Bible. Those who reject the Bible as a means of correction are usually the ones who need to hear the scriptures most. It is important, however, to use scripture in a time they will be willing to receive it.

It is never a good time to begin using Bible verses in the heat of an argument. At this time, each person is focused on how he or she can win the argument or at least feel like he or she has won. When we use the Bible then, it becomes the last-ditch effort for correction instead of the first method of change.

By bringing up issues that are biblically sinful and immoral, we have the opportunity to provide discipleship to people. This edifies them through correction. When we bring up amoral issues, we are placing judgment on them. Our opinions, culture, upbringing, and life experiences have helped shape who we are, but criticizing something because others are not like us or do not see things our way does not make it okay. When we let external influences other than the Bible dictate our perception of sin or inappropriate behavior, we are judging. When we let the Holy Spirit guide us using solid scriptural backing, we are prepared to disciple the person through inappropriate behaviors.

PRIVACY

The manner in which things are brought up will also show if the person is trying to help or judge someone. When we become so frustrated with an action, we will react in one of four ways:

1. We will ignore it, ultimately leading to passive-aggressive behaviors.
2. We will try to make it a public issue, thinking the more people who know about it, the more others will be able to help them with the issue.

3. They will gossip about it, never telling the person what they truly feel until he or she finds out through the rumor mill.

4. They will go to the person in private and talk with him or her about the issue in a sincere attempt to help.

The first three actions are the most common ways we address issues in society today. It has become socially acceptable to believe actions are more successful when more people are involved in the issue. It is the intervention concept of correction.

People gather those who might have some level of influence in the person's life and come up with a game plan to tell him or her of the inappropriate behavior. As they gather, each has an idea how the person's behavior has affected them, and each makes a plea for the behavior to stop.

Gathering others around us, we believe that strength in numbers will allow us to address issues in a way that will get the person to stop the behavior. It is not because all the people are providing influence at one time, but because each person addresses the behavior individually as if he or she has noticed something. The gossip and passive-aggressive approach seeks to accomplish this the most.

Public judgment makes every attempt to expose a person's behavior so other people know the person is struggling. This is malice, and damaging action can push people away from the church, isolate them in the workplace, and reject them from the family. This action extends beyond Matthew 18:15–17, which says, "If he pays no attention to them, tell the church."

When we are correcting someone, we are not telling him or her about how he or she has wronged us, but we are seeking an opportunity to disciple and mentor the person into a more appropriate behavior. Guiding someone is not designed to be a public action; it is private conversations among individuals with the expected outcome of change, not exposure.

As the instrument that God uses to change lives, we have to be cautious not to embarrass the person. Having the conversation in private with someone is the best way to affect change. If the situation has the potential of turning into an argument, it might be best for someone else to come alongside you during the discussion. It is important the other person is trustworthy and has the same or higher level of authority or trust in his or her life. If that does not happen, it would only seem if you were bringing someone else with you to gang up on him or her.

Our sensitivity to the issue will serve as the determining factor for growth and correction of the immoral behavior. If we fail to respect the other person's privacy in the issue, we have failed to provide biblical correction. Being concerned with his or her feelings in the action points toward correction, while complete disregard for the person reflects an attitude of judgment on him or her.

When we tell people they cannot judge us based on something we are doing, that conflicts with their point of view. It is important to be able to show them the love and compassion of Christ through correction, not judgment. This compassion only comes from speaking in a position of authority with the right attitude of love, with biblical backing, and in a private setting. When we are not able to accomplish these things, we really are placing judgment on them and not providing biblical correction.

It is not up to us to determine if people's actions are a direction from a relationship with God or personal desire. We have to remember that God will never guide you to do anything that would conflict with His mandates for Christian living. If you can appropriately back your correction with biblical teaching and have earnestly prayed over the issue, you can go into a conversation knowing that you will speak with the wisdom of God.

Praying over the issue also includes searching yourself. Understand why you feel it is necessary to correct the person. If you find that correcting the person would make you feel better, you might be placing judgment on him or her from personal opinion. If this is the case, you should take a few steps back and seek correction for yourself. "Take the log out of your eye," as Jesus instructs (Matt. 7:3–5).

Ultimately we have a responsibility to our Christian brothers and sisters to provide them with proper biblical correction. If we allow other Christians to live in sin, are we any better than they are for being bystanders of their behavior? We also have a responsibility to share the gospel message with others, but doing so does not always mean we expose others' sins. It means we share the love and truth of salvation through grace. Exposing sin is the work of the Holy Spirit's conviction, not our personal desire and opinion.

CHAPTER 3

SELF-REFLECTION OR SMALL GROUP DISCUSSION QUESTIONS

1. What experiences have you had where people have tried to give you correction but it came out as judgment?

2. What does it mean to you when Christ says you have to take the log out of your eye before you can remove the speck from another person's eye?

3. Have you ever experienced someone who became so upset with your attempt to correct him or her that he or she verbally or even physically attacked you?

4. How do you understand the difference between judgment and correction?

5. Who are the most important people that can speak with authority in your life?

6. Do you know what your spiritual gifting is and what God's calling in your life is? If so, what is it?

7. What attitudes do you take with those who frustrate you?

8. How often does your personality get in the way of providing biblical correction?

9. What does it feel like when you are corrected publicly?

10. When you are corrected publicly, how do you feel toward the person who gave the correction?

SESSION 5: TELL ME THE TRUTH

If there be no God, then what is truth but the average of all lies.

—Robert Brault

I enjoy speaking with people to figure out what makes them tick. Hearing about where they have been or what they have done interests me because it points to who they are now. Much of the time when I do this, I am not talking a lot but listening.

You can gain a great deal of knowledge and understanding about why people act certain ways. This is not something that most people are able to do, but many think they can do. To accurately evaluate people and make determinations on why they present certain behaviors takes years of education and experience. In the same respect, others have a natural ability to read people for who they are. Within either ability, there are those who have the uncanny ability to determine if someone is acting like someone he or she is not. Those who have this ability can also tell when someone is lying to them.

My wife, for example, can tell when someone is lying or read his or her character in a heartbeat. This is a huge blessing because she has given me sound advice in some difficult situations. This advice has warned me against people who I should watch out for and some who always seemed to be lying to me. There are instances where I didn't listen to her, and it has come back to bite me in the end.

The biggest benefits are catching those who lie to her. When she catches someone in a lie, she probes to find out why he or she has lied and what the real truth is. Despite the training I have, her natural ability has helped balance us out and saved me from many disasters. In a mixture of understanding my wife's natural ability and my education and background, it has become apparent to me that people lie often, and others misuse statements to get the truth.

Some people have such high stress when telling the truth that they develop a natural defense mechanism that causes them to lie in order to protect themselves from disappointing others or experiencing the rejection and pain they might feel from the past. I have counseled with people who believe, if they were going to hurt one way or another, telling half-truths or lying might get them out of trouble easier than simply telling the truth and taking responsibility for their actions. I know some people who feel that truth is relative and what we believe to be truth is reality. However, there are many who believe regardless of the response, "The truth will set you free."

This thought process is common when you think about it, the fact that truth is viewed as a relative statement for our society today. What we believe to be true is truth to us. Therefore, when we are faced with thought processes that go against what we believe, we consider it falsehood unless proven otherwise.

Those who oppose our thought processes will force people to see things their way with the philosophy that truth equates to freedom. In people who consistently receive repercussions for truth or lies, the truth rarely equated to freedom, only more strife and burden. For many of these people, statements like "The truth will set you free" are irrelevant social clichés.

I have heard "the truth will set you free" misused about as much as I have heard "God will never give you more than you can handle." Just as the latter statement is used to give encouragement through difficult times, our society has coined the association with truth and freedom in an attempt to inspire people to tell the truth.

There is freedom in truth, and people do feel more relieved when they have told the truth, but when this statement is compared to its biblical origin, we can see how it is misused. When the statement is made, rarely does anyone say, "The Bible says the truth will set you free." That is because many who use the phrase today really do not know that it is in the Bible. In fact, it is written in the Bible, word for word. In the second part of John

8:32, Jesus says to the people, "And the truth will set you free." The mistake people make is failing to look at the first part of the verse, let alone the context of the passage. Once again, society has taken a statement from the Bible and developed it into their truth.

As Christians, it is imperative that we understand what Christ intended when he said "The truth will set you free." By understanding this, we can then develop an understanding of why people lie, how the truth can actually set someone free, and how we achieve righteousness through forgiveness and truth. Before we can look at those aspects, it is equally important to know the effects of lying socially and personally.

While society believes truth to be relative, we have to look at the impact that lies will cause individuals. People do not escape the repercussion of truth or lies based on what they believe to be true, but what others believe is truth. When people face the emotional overload of holding on to a lie, the physical ailments associated with the stress or the spiritual emptiness of unforgiving lies that they become are desperate for freedom in their lament.

By telling the truth, you will be free of the burdens carried that often accompany a lie. This burden is more than emotional but extends to issues of consistency, memory, and broken relationships. When we think about the freedom we can have by telling the truth, there is great opportunity for respect, trustworthiness, and peace of mind.

When we tell a lie, we believe that what we are saying is going to fix the issues we might be facing. We lie because we think we can get away with it and we will not be caught in the situation that really lies before us. The emotional effects that become burdensome in the wake of our lies do and will create an emotional overload that fosters the growth of depression, worry, and anxiety.

Many people walk into my office with an overwhelming sense of emotional strife. It is apparent they have been carrying the baggage of their past for many years—lies they have told to stay out of trouble, lies they have told to make themselves more than what they are, and lies they have told to encourage themselves to be more, do more, and, most of all, fool more. And these lies have led them to depression, a feeling of hopelessness because there does not seem like a way back to the truth. They have held on to the lies so much they have forgotten who they really are. The depression they feel is overwhelming and exhausting, and weighs them down to the point of despair.

This despair leads to worry. There are two common types of worry: the healthy and unhealthy. Healthy worry will allow us to worry about something that we take seriously and do not want to make a mistake. For example, if someone wanted to ask his girlfriend to marry him and he was really worried about asking, he is worried because he is taking the next step in his relationship seriously. And he worries because it is a big commitment and he wants to ensure this person is the one. That is healthy worry.

Unhealthy worry will prevent us from doing something that we would normally be able to do. With unhealthy worry, we easily talk ourselves out of events and situations. Unhealthy worry transitions into anxiety issues because it prevents us from doing the things we can and should do because of unrealistic expectations of disaster.

While worry and anxiety are often associated with each other, the two are very different. Anxiety has the characteristic that debilitates people and prevents them from living a normal life because of irrational thoughts in various situations. On the other hand, worry consumes a person and plays a major factor in the decision-making process that can control our response to situations.

Worry easily causes us to lie or come to terms with our fear and tell the truth. Some might even call it conviction when we worry about something so much that we confess to the wrongdoing. When people live with and in lies, they have a constant underlying worry. The worry carries with it the responsibility of eventually telling the truth, the truth coming out somehow, or even being caught (Luke 12:2–3).

The emotional impact of lying holds horrible consequences that can weigh down one's ability to feel lifted from the burdens of life. Telling a lie creates a chain reaction that will perpetuate into higher levels of stress. With higher levels of stress, it becomes a well-known fact that physiological effects take their toll on the body.

It is common knowledge that stress leads to high blood pressure, heart disease, and other physiological impacts. Lately numerous studies show that stress leads to obesity and unwanted belly fat. It is up to you to determine if a lie, even compounded white lies, is worth the extra emotional weight, not to mention the extra physical weight.

Since I am not a doctor, I encourage you, the reader, to look into the physical effects of stress in your life. While we think that a simple lie will not bother us and we see no impact from our stress, we might see no issues with telling a lie. If you are not carrying around the emotional impact of living with a lie, you are experiencing the negative spiritual influence that lying causes.

The simple fact is that emotional and physical impact causes something within our bodies that have a tangible impact. Conviction over lying to others has a spiritual impact as well. When we hold onto lies, we create a divide that inhibits forgiveness between God and us.

The thought that our lies toward other people can prevent God's forgiveness is hard to believe. After all, we serve an all-forgiving God whose grace and mercy abounds in all our transgressions, but the issue is not that God withholds forgiveness because we lied, but He withholds forgiveness because we have not sought true repentance. The repentance that is essential for God to forgive is essential for us to be forgiven by others.

We have to approach God and others with a repentant heart that confesses our wrongdoing. We cannot approach God as if we have no sin in our lives and expect His Word to be in us (1 John 1:8–10). To think it is okay to lie and then move forward with our Christian walk causes us to deceive ourselves as much as it does the other person. The deception of ourselves is what changes who we are before God and man. This same deception puts us in emotional, physical, and spiritual bondage that changes the very essence of who God created us to be.

If we are created to be people who live and act in the image of God, then we are people who should be despised by lies and offended by the thought of deceiving other people into believing we are someone who is above reproach. More so, if we believe our lies are not harming our relationships with others and our relationship with God, then we are mistaken by the power of truth in our lives.

The question then becomes, "What is the benefit of lying if it will only lead to more distress?" It is apparent the negative impact of a lie will be far more damaging than the positive impacts of the truth. If we feel the need to lie in order to avoid responsibility, feelings of failure, or personal disappointment, we have turned to a society that places more significance on masquerade than trustworthiness.

Looking at the Context

The development of any relationship with others is based on trust. We have to trust the people we are with in order to have a relationship with them. Trust is having the faith they will be honest, act with integrity, and be who they really are despite the circumstances. While our trustworthiness establishes the freedom to be who God made us to be, Jesus was not referring to the necessity of telling the truth when he addresses the issue in his teaching.

When looking at the passage in the book of John that describes truth and freedom, we find the stark difference in what Christ is referring to when He says the truth will set you free (John 8:31–47). The simple thought of just telling the truth or even confessing your wrongdoings is customary, but essentially cliché in context of this scripture.

In the preceding verses that describe truth and freedom, Jesus relays the differences between the rest of the world and Him (John 8:23–24). It is imperative that people understand He is the Son of God. He does this by making "you and I" statements. The contrast given in these statements can be hard for some to believe. This is why Christ has created within each of us the choice of belief or disbelief based on our own understanding.

If we were to believe that Christ is the Son of God, we would have eternal life, but if we have disbelief, we would not receive entrance into the kingdom of heaven. If we do not believe that Christ is the way, the truth, and the life (John 14:6), we have negated the very essence of who Christ is and how He plays a role in the salvation of all people. Our disbelief prevents us from understanding Christ's importance in our own lives, let alone the overarching concept of the Trinity.

Our understanding of the Trinity is not about what Christ is, but who Christ is. The concept goes beyond just hearing the gospel, but living the gospel in a continued active message through our actions, deeds, and words. As we look at the freedom we find in truth, the context draws the reader into issues of how Christ becomes involved in our everyday lives and how we serve God within the freedom Christ provides.

Jesus's True Disciples

A disciple is someone who follows the teaching of another person. Notice they are not people who hear the teachings of someone but actually adapts them to their life and adheres to the teaching through action. The concepts, values, and ideals are relayed in their everyday lives.

There are people who are disciples of false teachers, even in the Christian faith. These people adapt to the teachings of pastors who take a preferred theology and have them follow that theology despite the way it negates biblical mandates. They will skew biblical teachings into what they want them to mean in order to be more accepting, inclusive, and adaptive to a sinful society that changes its perception of right and wrong on a daily basis.

Because some of these pastors are skilled speakers and can formulate excellent expositions that make sense, they are able to manipulate the scriptures in a way that is believable. Unfortunately, when this happens, these false teachers persuade people to believe lies, and the hearer ultimately argues the lie as if it is truth. As stated in the introduction, it is not because they want to make people believe the lie out of knowledge, but because they want to help people believe in a way they were unknowingly persuaded to believe.

Just as much as there are false teachers in the world today, there are also false disciples in the world too. When we encounter these false disciples, we have to be prepared to show them the truth through scripture and context.

Our desire to follow what we understand as truth makes us real disciples, no matter if it is right or wrong. In the same respect, when we look at our lives and what we truly desire, we have to look for someone to disciple, teach, mentor, and, in the midst of that, give us a direction in life that will allow us to continue in a life worthy of living. The life worth living is found in truth.

Jesus says in John 8:31 that if we are really his disciples, we will continue in His Word. This does not mean that we are challenged to simply hear His Word or take it in so we can teach other people, but to live it out. We are not called to simply exist in the kingdom of God, but each of us has a purpose that he or she must live out.

As the author of Hebrews relays, we are running a race, and we have to run the race until we have crossed the finish line (Heb. 12:1b). We must keep our eyes on Jesus (Heb. 12:2a), and by doing so, we are given the strength to continue in our Christian walk.

When Jesus is talking about continuing in His Word, He is saying that believers must abide in His teachings and not deviate from the discipleship He provided. Within this instruction, it is vitally important that all believers be good stewards of the scriptures. Since all of us have a responsibility to focus on Jesus and His teachings, we have an obligation to continue in these teachings by following them without making changes that adapt to our thought processes or social pressures.

This means that, as Christians, we are obligated to transform ourselves from what we want to what Christ wants in us. We cannot serve the kingdom of God if we are more worried about achieving our own agendas and labeling them as kingdom objectives.

The Freedom of Truth

If we were to follow the teaching of Christ as an obligation of the Christian life, it would be easy for us to think Christianity is more constraining than it is a freedom-giving dedication. In John 8:32, Christ says that knowing the truth will set us free.

Freedom comes from knowing the truth, and as Christ later says to His disciples, He is the truth. People who believe that being a Christian provides more bondage than it does freedom don't know the truth well enough to find freedom in Christ.

Putting verse 31 and 32 together, we can see that being a disciple of Christ means that we get to know who He is, and when we know who He is, we find a deeper level of freedom because we don't miss Christ for the standards but follow the standards because of our adoration of Christ.

Knowing the truth is higher than the burden of knowledge. Many people know the standards and choose not to follow them. They believe the standards of Christianity are too hard to follow and freedom to act and do what they want will result in a level of happiness. The unfortunate thing is that I rarely counsel people who are chasing after Christ. Instead I am counseling people who are trying to find fulfillment in sinful behaviors and fail to find everlasting happiness.

These sinful behaviors cause people to continue searching for the same feeling they got the last time they engaged in them. The drunk needs more to feel the buzz, the drug addict takes more to feel the high, and the sex addict needs more to feel the pleasure. Most sin issues people engage in will always leave people with a desire, even a need, for more to feel the same as they did the first time. This places them in a level of bondage that consumes their life with chasing after something they will never feel again. They are continually left empty and wanting.

On the other hand, those who know Christ find the freedom to live life without the insatiable need and desires of the world. When we know Christ as the truth, we search the Bible for answers, we pray to know and understand God, we have relationships that grow and develop over time, and each time we know God more, we get a different feeling. Our joy becomes complete in Christ. We learn that things of this world are momentary and Christ is eternal.

Knowing the truth represents our faith in Christ, our faith represents belief, and belief empowers confidence to live the next day, hour, and minute of our lives. Faith gives us hope for the things that we cannot see. If we cannot see them, we have to believe they exist. As Christians, we have to believe that God will take care of us. If we believe God will take care of us, we can have the confidence to go through life while taking on challenges in our walk. We face the issues that surround our society today with a level of forgiveness because we know we too have been forgiven.

This confidence gives us freedom because we are not bound by sin, regret, and, most of all, the things of the flesh, including death. It allows us to live in the freedom of Christ that gives confidence in the reality that every temptation that comes our way will always lead to a way out, and when we do fall to sin, we are forgiven. The forgiving grace of the Holy Spirit will lift the need for us to carry our past transgressions because Christ will lift those burdens from us. And when we find the freedom from sin and transgressions, we realize we are no longer slaves chasing after hopeless desires, but we are serving an Almighty God who gives us purpose and direction.

THE SLAVE AND THE SERVANT

Defining freedom is always interesting. Different people have different views of freedom. When I do marriage counseling, I often hear, "I just want my freedom back." Our society today equates freedom with being able to anything we want to do without repercussion. The unfortunate part about that is that freedom has a higher responsibility. Even with the most liberal of freedoms comes rules and guidelines.

True freedom means you have a future hope and everything you work for has a purpose. Every trial and tribulation you face in life has meaning. This means that, when you find freedom, your service to something greater than yourself does not go without blessing. This is not to be confused with prosperity because sometimes the blessing is the eternal joy of belonging to God and the peace of being in His will.

The people began to question Jesus because they did not understand the difference between enslavement to their sinful behaviors and the enslavement to man (John 8:33). They only equated slavery with the enslavement of the Jewish people in Egypt. However, Christ was not referring to the bondage of man, but the bondage of sin.

In verse 34, Christ says, "I assure you: Everyone who commits a sin is a slave of sin." This means that every person is enslaved to the power of sin in his or her life. It holds us captive and prevents us from knowing true freedom. This is the paramount statement for everyone to understand. Christ is the truth, and He, being the truth, sets you free from your sin.

We can resist sin issues, but we will fall to our fleshly desires no matter how hard we try. The only way to be completely freed from sinful desire is to find Christ in our lives and continually seek His truth. This is the difference from being a slave to sin and a servant of the Lord.

A slave master demands work out of his people, and if the work is not done, then he punishes them with brutality. The emotional and physical effects of our sinful desires will punish every aspect of our lives. We labor and toil for the moment, we become consumed with the pursuit of our sinful nature, and ultimately we are swallowed up in the struggle with no humanly hope to redeem or recover from the depths of the hole we have dug. In most cases, because we have no idea we have dug such a deep hole until we look up and realize there is no way out, we are trapped. That is what slavery in our sin looks like, hopelessness.

Servanthood is the ability to work for something without the expectation of payment. Those who are enslaved by sin have the expectation of the emotional or physical return on their behavior. Those who serve have the expectation that their master is glorified and reflected in their behavior. Most churches do not demand labor and toil of their congregations, and if you find a church that does, you are in the wrong church.

It is essential for people to find a church that demands kingdom service. Kingdom service is different from being enslaved by the congregation. Those who are in kingdom service joyfully work in the nursery, are willing to serve on the prayer team, and even go into the community as part of the evangelism program of the church. The difference is their desire to serve the Lord instead of the church's desire to cover a program because they cannot let the church down the street have a program they do not have.

Many of our churches today are covered with people who are enslaved in programming. Their attitudes show it. When my family and I visit churches all around the nation, it is interesting to see how people react. You can tell the ones who are doing things for the Lord and those who are "forced" ministry workers.

In some of the churches, we cannot get past the greeter without a genuine desire to know who we are and where we came from, even if we are just passing through. You can see the joy of the Lord in how they approach their responsibility to the kingdom. While in other churches we visit, we ask if there is a children's program, and the greeter rolls his or her eyes and haphazardly points in a general direction as if it is a burden he or she is even there.

When you attend a church and encounter volunteers, you can see who feels the church has enslaved them and who has been given freedom in the Lord. They are serving with great pride to ensure the kingdom of God is reflected to everyone with the love and compassion each of us are commanded to give.

Differentiating between being slaves or servants helps us develop an understanding regarding whom we serve. In the following verses (John 8:35–44) of this passage, Christ becomes very bold in his expression of which people serve. It is a good reminder for all people to ask the question, "Who is my master?"

When Jesus begins to talk to the people, he relays the message of the Father. The Jewish people saw their father to be Abraham, and Jesus quickly states that there is only one Father, God. If they were like Abraham though, they would listen to God, just as Abraham did. If they listened to

God, then they would know that Jesus was the Son of God. But instead of listening to God, seeing Jesus as the truth, and hearing what Jesus was saying as truth, they were trying to kill Jesus. This behavior was not reflective of God, but reflective of the devil.

We have to understand the truth of who we are as people is a reflection of the things and people who influence our lives. If we are not willing to break the mold of the negative influence, then we will not be willing to live our lives in a way that reflects Jesus as the truth that sets us free.

Christ is saying that if God were their Father, not only would they recognize Jesus as truth, but also they would be able to understand the freedom He is able to give. Because the people did not recognize Him as truth, they did not listen to Him or what He had to say (John 8:46). If they were not willing to listen to God, then He could not be their Father because they were not from God (John 8:47).

As Christians, we have to believe and have faith that Christ is the Son of God, and we have to listen to the Word of God. It is not simply reading or hearing the Word of God. It is living in the Word. It was not a matter of Jesus's teaching being a suggestion for the people to follow, but His teaching was the paramount aspect of understanding how to live as a Christian.

Reading the Bible and listening to the voice of God in the various ways He speaks to His people are fundamental aspects of spiritual growth. We have to be confident we know what God is asking us to do and then be able to carry it out until the task is complete. If we are confident in knowing what God has called us to do, then we will have faith in living out our purpose in God.

When we search for the purpose in life, it is easy to fall to sin because we do not have the confidence level that what we are doing gives us purpose. People search for purpose in all aspects of their lives. Purpose is often associated with success and status. The more vocational success we have or the greater our social status, thus creating a greater purpose in our lives according to social and societal norms. Unfortunately, achieving those things outside of dependence on the hope and truth of Jesus only leads to acceptance of sinful behavior.

Sinful behavior will continually leave you wanting. We take on the mantra that if we only had the next best thing, people would like us more, or, even worse, we would like ourselves more. Ultimately we live a lie, tell lies to get there, and compromise our Christian values to impress society and validate ourselves. As I have said before, this only leaves us in bondage. The hope and truth of Jesus is that we have eternal salvation, a freedom found in the message of the cross.

When we believe the message of the cross and we have hope in the things to come, we are free because the worry and sting of death no longer has control over us. Jesus holds the key to our freedom, and through that freedom, we walk with a new level of courage, believing that what once held us captive in the past no longer has power or control in our lives.

We understand from looking at this passage in context that Jesus is not teaching us to tell the truth, but to believe the truth through salvation in Him. Through His truth, we are given freedom from the bondage of sin, not encapsulated by the emotional strife of dishonest, immoral behavior.

WHAT WE SHOULD USE INSTEAD

"If Jesus were not talking about telling the truth but being the truth, then how do we combat the liar?" The question was asked when I taught this class in a seminar. This is a valid question people can ask, especially when our society is full of people who lie. Our white lies, secrets, and social deceptions hurt our relationships as much as our desire to be brutally honest in what we say and do.

I have always found it interesting that, when other people lie to us, we will get very upset. Yet they have no issues lying to someone else. In fact, some will get so upset when they catch someone lying to them that they would be more willing to sever the relationship than try to reconcile the differences. The feeling of being betrayed by others is much stronger than the feeling of betraying others. Without Jesus and the Holy Spirit's conviction, our willingness to betray others has no level of accountability until we are caught.

When it comes to combating a liar though, we have to understand the only person we are responsible for is ourselves. You can only evaluate your own life and live as an example for them to follow. When given the opportunity, mentor and develop them through knowledge of why it is important to be honest and truthful in what we do.

Why Do People Lie

In order to understand the issues surrounding lies, we have to address the question, "Why do people lie?" There is always a reason unless the person has serious psychological issues that only a professional counselor can address. The reasoning varies based on the motives of the person. What motivates us will always dictate our response to things. For example, if money is our motivator, we will do what it takes to have more money. If promotion is our motivator, we will do what it takes to be promoted. If relationship with certain people, groups, or classes becomes our motivator, then we will do what it takes to have relationship with those people.

Regardless of our motivation, there is a top-nine list of reasons why we feel the need to lie in order to achieve our goals. This list is not exhaustive and represents my experiences in the counseling room.

1. **To hide wrongdoing**. This has to be the most common form of lying that I have seen. We do not want to let people know we are not perfect. It's funny though because the Bible constantly reminds us that we are not perfect. That is why we have the need for Jesus. Our imperfections make us who we are. If it were not for the things others find as imperfect, then we would all be the same. There are valid mistakes in this world, and these should be accepted, discussed, and forgiven. After all, God has forgiven you for things you have done that you don't deserve.

   a. We first hide our wrongdoing because, while God will forgive us, most people are not willing to. In my experience, people don't want to forgive others, or they try to hide their wrongdoing because, when they seek forgiveness, they feel the road to restoration is too difficult. In this case, we tend to forget that any road worth taking is not an easy one. The most difficult roads are those that bring the most satisfaction when we are finished traveling them. Always be willing to travel the difficult road.

   b. We also hide our wrongdoing because of social perceptions. So many people believe, because they perform tasks with precision, others must perform at the same but not higher level. Note that I did not say perform tasks with perfection. No one can complete a task without perfection. I learned this while performing military funeral honors with the air force. One of the most difficult aspects to providing honors is the firing party. It requires three to five people moving in perfect unity so each person firing the weapon will only make the sound of one shot. Imagine the hours of practice it takes to make one charging click, one bang, and one movement. However, no matter how perfect we thought we did, our leader would always have a critique for us. His goal was not to make us feel defeated but to make us strive for better. There was no way we could lie about our performance because the performance was not just one person. It was a combination of people moving in unison. Just as we each have a personal responsibility in life, the total performance in life is a combination of the people who surround us. When we make mistakes, we have to try to stop hiding our wrongdoings. While our honor guard leader would point out our wrongdoings, everyone would begin to point and blame the other for the mistake. The desire to hide the wrongdoing became more important than the desire to become better. When we encounter people who desire to hide their wrongdoing, we have to remember they also have a lack of desire to become personally better and will usually blame someone else for their imperfections.

2. **To avoid disappointing others**. We all want for others to like and accept us. Even when we do not like someone, we want him or her to like us. Some will say they do not care, but in reality they probably care more. It is a natural instinct because we were created for relationship, and when we want a relationship with someone, we will work as hard as we can to have that relationship. Remember the heart's desire. At the root of every heart's desire is to achieve these goals with some company. No one wants to be lonely because he or she does not want to have to celebrate alone. We are so afraid of disappointing others because we are afraid of being alone in

most cases. This is a concept developed for many at a young age. Parents show disappointment in their children in multiple ways. Some will just come out and say it, "I'm very disappointed in you." On the other hand, a few will show disappointment in physical punishment. Regardless, the greater the need for relationship, the greater one might be willing to lie in order to impress. This goes hand-in-hand with hiding our wrongdoings. Sometimes we lie just so we are not blamed for something, but in many cases, we do not want to disappoint those we revere. As we get older, we have ingrained in our thought processes that if we disappoint people we revere, we will lose our relationship with them. The issue is that they also think that, when they are disappointed, they should sever the relationship. The result is people who tell lies and try to avoid every bit of disappointment they can in order to keep their relationships with others. As long as people have personal expectations for others, they will be disappointed. When we try to minimize the amount of lies that people tell us, we have to minimize the amount of disappointment we have in them. By letting people know that it is okay to make mistakes, we are letting them know their shortcomings are forgivable. We have to be willing to stop being disappointed in ourselves and be ready to change people with love and forgiveness rather than reprimanding them with disappointment and regret.

3. **To impress others.** I have two friends who are avid fishermen, and they love to take pictures of the fish they caught and text them to each other. They do this to avoid the "I got a bigger fish than you" story. Back before we all carried the all-in-one phones and cameras, we could tell anyone a "fish story," and each time we told it, it seemed the fish got bigger and bigger. You might ask why. It was because we wanted to impress our friends. Hunters saw the fifteen-point buck but did not shoot it out of respect. Workers would have taken the VP promotion but did not want the responsibility. This list goes on and on about who or what we wish we would be and what we really are. When we tell lies to impress others, once again, a status statement lets people know we are not

inept. In some cases, it is to try to make people think we are better than they are, but in most, it is to make people think we are better than what we think we are. Notice I did not say to make people think we are better than they think we are. This is because often people want to be like the people they revere. They will begin dressing and talking like them and making fun of others who they used to be friends with to cover up who they really are because of who they want to be. The unfortunate thing is that people lie so much to be someone else that they lose their identity. If you have to lie to yourself so much about who you are to a group of people that you lose your identity, then that group of people is not worth hanging out with. That statement sounds wonderful when you read it, but it is most difficult when you try to put it into practice. In order to be accepted by groups, we think we have to conform to whom they are instead of being the unique puzzle piece that fits into place within the groups we can be part of. Paul is a wonderful example of this when the three testimonies of his conversion is recorded in Acts (Acts 9:1–9, 22:6–21, 26:12–23). Some would say he changed his message; therefore, the story has no integrity. However, if you look at the accounts, the message never changes. The delivery does. Paul never compromised whom he was in order to fit in, but he understood how to live the truth of who he was within multiple cultures and environments. We do not need to overinflate our lives to impress others or ourselves. We need to find a way to fit into different cultures within the story that God gave us. Simply put, if you want to tell the best fish story, go catch the biggest fish, and then you will have the story to tell.

4. **To avoid consequences**. When a parent asks his or her child if he or she stole a cookie from the cookie jar, the child's immediate response is usually, "No, I didn't do it." Funny how we can tell a lie so quick when we are questioned about wrongdoing. When that child took the cookie, he or she was not thinking about how to lie about it. All he or she was thinking was that he or she wanted a cookie. When the child sees his or her parent is so upset with him or her, he or she immediately goes to self-preservation mode and

tells a lie to avoid the consequences. As we get older, we begin to do things with a thought of how to cover up our mistakes. Just as I wrote previously, we have a natural desire to hide our wrongdoing as well as impress others. However, sometimes it is impossible to hide the wrongdoing; therefore, we tell lies in order to avoid more severe discipline. When I was eighteen, I visited a local Christian college. On my way home, I got pulled over for speeding. Since my car window did not roll down, I was sitting in the police cruiser as the officer wrote the ticket. I asked him how the radar gun works and talked about how I was interested in what he did. In reality I did not care about the radar gun. All I wanted was to divert his attention to get out of the ticket. There was no denying I was speeding, so I lied about my interest in order to be nice, and hopefully he would return the favor. Since I was a captive audience, he returned the favor. Once he completed writing my ticket for speeding, he spent about fifteen minutes telling me how the radar works. Not only did I have to pay the consequence for speeding; I paid the consequence for my lie when I acted as if I really cared about how a radar gun worked. When we fear the consequence more than we fear the fallout of our lie, we might end up spending more time trying to fix our damage. We have to be willing to take responsibility for our actions despite what the consequence might be. If we are not willing to take the good and bad results, we should not be willing to carry out the action.

5. **To avoid doing things we don't like**. I do not like onions. I know they add flavor, but in most cases, I have to force myself to eat them. This has created two issues where lies are involved. Because my children know I order things without onions, they inherently do not like onions either. The issue is that they are clueless as to why they do not like onions. Because my wife is allergic to shellfish and she doesn't eat it, they just tell people they are allergic to onions. When they say this, people will not give them onions and be extra cautious when preparing their food. In a way, it is funny, but they are now old enough to know they are not allergic to onions. Otherwise we would have killed them a long time ago

with our cooking. This is a cute example of how we lie to avoid doing things we do not like, but there are times in our lives that we lie because we just don't want to do something. Our boss gives us voluntary overtime, and we say no because we have that thing to do that would not allow us. In reality, how many times have you said, "Gee, I'd love to but ..." Would you really love to do what they ask of you, or would you rather say, "I can't because I really don't want to." Our society has created a social courtesy to let people down with grace. If not, we become offended and feel the person is treating us unfair. What becomes overwhelming is the amount of couples that will not be honest with each other and have list after list of reasons not to do something for their spouse. These couples will continually lie to each other in an attempt to avoid participating in various events. Telling lies to avoid doing something is simply giving excuses that have no valid reasoning. It compromises your integrity and changes the way people think of you. We have to understand that, in order to build a reputation of being trustworthy with anything, we have to resist telling lies in order to avoid doing things we don't like to do.

6. **To hide personal shortcomings**. This form of lying is one of the most common. Though we hate to admit it, we all recognize our shortcomings. Sometimes these come in the form of sin issues, but regardless of the personal defect, people are more willing to lie due to their shortcomings. When I was younger, I remember seeing someone with a shirt that said, "I'm not normal." I remember asking the person what normal was. When you think about it, there are all kinds of normal. There is social/cultural normal, personal normal, or even family normal. This concept of normal will define our shortcomings. Just like normal is relative to the person defining it, the concept of shortcomings are relative to the person experiencing them. This is why so many people are willing to lie about their shortcomings. Paired with the shortcoming is the perception of perfection. There are those who want to portray themselves as something better than what they are. This concept goes beyond the need to impress someone but translates into a deeper level of

self-image. When we are in a different situation or one where the expectations dictate we do not show our imperfections, we show a different side of ourselves that reflects the lies we tell. The best example of this is for the Christian believer who comes to church and talks about sin issues being unacceptable. He or she talks about God's mercy for the occasional sin but will not address the addictive behaviors of sin that consume his or her life. The uncontrollable need to submit to significant addictive behaviors were, in certain communities, considered acceptable, but in the church community, the behaviors are not. We call this hypocritical behavior, but when it comes down to it, we have to decide which community we want to be part of and live that lifestyle, even if it means rejecting another community that deems our inappropriate behaviors as normal. To go into communities lying to others about our shortcomings results in us lying to ourselves about our belief systems, spiritually and morally.

7. **To shut people up**. I know a person who will tell you everything you want to hear and very rarely the truth of what you need to hear. Worse, he agrees to everything. He might not know how to execute or even what you are saying sometimes because he just does not care. His goal is to shut you up so he can move on to the next thing. People will tell lies in order to shut other people up. They might not intend to do what they are being asked of, or they might not have any idea of how to do what they are being taught, but they will tell you they do in order to get you to stop giving directions and move on to making it happen. We all know people like this or even have been this person. We become so excited about something that we try to shut people up in order to get to what we want to do. It is a simple concept, if we agree with it or tell people we know the answers. And then we are able to get to the process we wanted to. It is like learning a new task and agreeing with the trainer but not really knowing how to do the task. On the other hand, there is the person who agrees to everything when he or she is being reprimanded in order avoid an argument. Married couples are notorious for this when they know a discussion can

lead to an argument. One person in the relationship will admit fault even when he or she is not guilty. As well, he or she will agree to change even when he or she does not have any intention to make the change in his or her life. When we are willing to lie to make people quiet, we fail to learn and grow in our lives. This growth can only happen from listening and learning from those who are commissioned to teach us. Missed opportunities to learn can and usually does lead to mistakes. It is important that we learn the entire process so we avoid mistakes, but also gain the knowledge to improve the processes that advance our situations and ourselves.

8. **We don't know what else to say**. People who do not know what to say will sometimes tell a lie in order to say something. When stories are being told and the person wants to feel like he or she is part of the group, the individual might tell lies to make people think he or she has had similar experiences in life. It's like my parents used to say, "If you don't have anything to say, don't say anything at all." As a society, we like to talk. Noise is something we have to have. So many people who live in a fast-paced life become uncomfortable when there is silence. When I am in counseling sessions, people do not like to be in silence. Pausing to allow people the opportunity to reflect can make them feel uncomfortable. Self-reflection can be even more awkward if we are not willing to confront our innermost thoughts. In order to avoid this, people will lie to divert attention from their true feelings. We have to remember that silence is better than lying. There is no other option when we are in a group of people than to be whom we are. Telling lies to fit in or break silence is another way to destroy our reputation. People will accept you more if you are silent but present than they would if you told stories just to be heard.

9. **To avoid spiritual corruption**. The last reason people lie is a culmination of all the reasons. Spiritual corruption is when we have taken our eyes off God to the extent that we lie to ourselves regarding our spiritual lives. We see these people in the church all the time, the ones who believe their attendance will grant them

109

admittance into the kingdom of heaven. Their misguided theologies will result in behaviors that are damaging to the soul. People who take their eyes off God will lie to their Christian friends and those who question their actions. They will always have an excuse as to why they were not able to consistently resist temptation. They have succumbed to the desire of their flesh because they have not covered themselves in the protection of God. In order to avoid spiritual corruption and lying about your faith, it is important for one to keep his or her eyes on Christ. Our dependence must be on the Word of God and His protection instead of the pleasures of this world that can destroy our relationship with God.

LYING IS A SIN

It is easy for us to say that lying is bad. Even looking at the list above regarding why people lie, we can see the negative impact that lying can have. It affects both the liar and victim. Besides breaking a set of moral codes that will compromise integrity in many situations, it violates one's trust and relationship with God's system of sinful behaviors against Him.

We have to remember when we commit a sinful act. It is against our bodies, but even more, we have broken a code of behavior against God. For Christians, they follow the holy scriptures for guidance and direction. Regardless of social acceptance of certain behaviors, the Christian must go to the Bible for direction. At that point, the Christian will begin to understand how he or she must change his or her life in order to become righteous in the eyes of God.

Lying, simply put, is sinful, and we can look toward the scripture to understand that. First, the Ten Commandments denote lying as a violation of God's code for His people. The ninth commandment states, "You shall not bear false testimony against your neighbor" (Ex. 20:16). This can mean two things. First, we do not lie with the intent to deceive our neighbor. Speaking against our neighbor in way that would discredit him or her under false pretenses is the second meaning for bearing false witness.

Most people see the latter as the definition of bearing false witness. They believe that telling a lie to someone is sinful behavior and against the Ten Commandments. The issue does not stop there according to the meaning of bearing false witness because speaking in a way that falsely discredits another person is still lying and considered a sinful action.

Our behaviors within the Ten Commandments are easily arguable. While we learn about them in our early Christian growth, some will say they are under the old covenant and modern Christianity is under the new covenant. If we follow the Ten Commandments, we need to make ourselves subject to all the other Old Testament laws. We learn, however, a lying tongue is one of the seven abominations toward God (Prov. 6:17).

God does not change His mind on what we should or should not do based on the covenant under which we fall. He only changes the level of grace in which He extends his mercy. While the Ten Commandments were given to the Israelites as a set of guidelines, the sinful nature that angers God has not changed. Similar to the Ten Commandments are the "Two Commandments" (Matt. 22:37–40). As Christ describes these two commandments, verse 40 affirms, "All the Law and the Prophets depend on these two commands."

When we connect the two, it is impossible to love your neighbor and deceive him or her at the same time. Likewise, it is impossible to love your neighbor and discredit him or her with falsehoods. Therefore if we transition into a new covenantal understanding of the law, we find that love for one's neighbor is synonymously the same requirement for God's people.

Simply put, a lying tongue is a sinful transgression against others that ultimately angers God. Paul affirms this in his letter to the Colossians when he writes, "Do not lie to one another, since you have put off the old self with its practices and have put on the new self" (Col. 3:9–10a).

When people become Christians, they are shedding the spirit of the old self. The desires, tactics, and attitudes in which they conducted themselves are invalid. There is a new self that emerges from the power of the Holy Spirit. This new self is what Christians depend on for strength in difficult situations because the new self is weak and can only be strengthened by the indwelling of the Holy Spirit.

When we lie, the new self should feel ashamed and outraged at lying and lies. This seems far-fetched, but if a Christian is truly yielding to the Holy Spirit, the very Spirit of God, and God is angered by sin, then the Holy Spirit should well up in believers. They should allow their displeasure to manifest itself in an anger that is not full of wrath, malice, and revenge (Col. 3:8), but full of love, mercy, and grace that does not tolerate abominations toward God.

As a society, we have begun to tolerate the abominations toward God that prevent us from standing firm against sin issues. As a society, we have to get back to where we were intolerant against sin and tolerant toward the sinner. Social acceptance has fallen into a trap that asserts the belief of loving the sinner means accepting the sin, and that is not what God intended.

We have to understand that acceptance of the sin in order to love the sinner is against the righteous behavior we should exhibit as a Christian. These laws were not written because we live in a righteous society that is without sin, but every law is written for "the lawless and rebellious, for the ungodly and sinful, for the unholy and irreverent" (1 Tim. 1:9). The interesting part of the 1 Timothy passage is that Paul begins to list murderers, sexually immoral, liars, and perjurers (1 Tim. 1:10). Anything contrary to sound teaching is considered lawless, and anyone who seeks to please the world through tolerance of his or her sin rejects sound teaching.

Rejecting the sound teaching of the gospel leads to rejection of God's desire for your life. Lying, as simple as it may seem, will imprison you in one of the easiest sinful behaviors a person can experience. While the lie is easy, monetarily cheap, and seemingly safe, it is the hardest, most emotionally expensive, and dangerous behavior one can commit. Emotionally trustworthy actions are the hardest situations to recover from; therefore, the sinful nature of a lie is destructive on multiple levels that one would never see until it is too late.

THE TRUTH DEVELOPS RIGHTEOUSNESS

Renewal of your spirit after lying is difficult. In fact, it is so difficult that many people would rather sever a relationship before they would reconcile and go through the difficult process of regaining trust.

It is the same way with God. People are more willing to avoid or suppress their sin issue than they are to confess their sin to God in order to find restoration. Interestingly enough, God knows every aspect of our heart. He knows the unforgiven lies we have told, and He knows the unresolved sin issues we hide from those who keep us accountable.

As Christians, we have shed our old selves, and we have put behind us our former way of life (Eph. 4:22). The former way of life is based in deceitful desires that fool us into believing that our lives are fine without God. However, when the Holy Spirit convicts us, we begin to learn that our old selves are a lie. We are not okay without God because He is the essence of the very breath we take.

No one can experience righteousness without the purity of truth (Eph. 4:24). This is a concept that allows us to understand that, in order to be more like God, we have to get closer to the truth of God. Too many people are willing to compromise the integrity of the Bible in order to fit into the preferred theology of today's society. By doing so, they are not attempting to get closer to the truth of who God is and what His desire for our lives is, but they are slowly staggering away from truth.

The distortion of what a new self looks like within the likeness of God creates the socially dysfunctional truth we see in today's society. Being made new in Christ requires us to speak truth, turn our back on lying, and realize we are members of one another (Eph. 4:25).

To be a member of one another, we have to look at it as being a single cell in the body of Christ. Each cell is joined together, making parts of the body, which has a specific function in the kingdom of God. The redeeming blood of Jesus feeds us all. When one cell in the body becomes corrupt, the body should do everything in its power to restore that cell.

In order to be restored to righteousness, we are not called to slander other people, but we are called to protect them and help them heal by picking up the pace and bearing one another's burdens as he or she heals from the wounds of his or her afflictions. When lying and deceit are involved, it is difficult to speak truth, and we are not able to put away the lying that will not only corrupt one part of the body but destroy the entire corpus.

Righteousness is pursuing the purity of truth through salvation in the living God. The pursuit of truth can only be obtained through a relationship with God and trusting Him for what He has done in your life as well as what He promises to do in your eternity. When we live in the confidence of our righteousness through God, we have no reason to lie because we are protected, guided, and convicted by the purist of truths, God.

TRUTH

As previously stated, there are many benefits to telling the truth. In order to sum these benefits into one thought process, below is an acronym that might help people remember to tell the truth:

- Trustworthy: People will entrust you with more when they know you are truthful.
- Reputable: A reputation for telling the truth builds confidence in your persuasive abilities.
- Understanding: People are more compassionate when the truth is told from the beginning.
- Transmittable: Telling the truth is contagious. Others will display the same integrity you have if you are willing to lead the way.
- Healthy: Clinically speaking, the truth will lower psychological disorders, physiologic conditions, and spiritual roadblocks.

Truth does provide some level of freedom from overpowering burdens. We have to remember that, when Christ made this statement, he was referring to the truth of salvation setting us free from the spiritual death that takes place without the reconciliation of sin in our lives. The truth of salvation will set you free from the bondage of sin just as much as telling the truth will free you from the bondage of your past regrets.

CHAPTER 4

SELF-REFLECTION OR SMALL GROUP DISCUSSION QUESTIONS

1. When you hear "the truth will set you free," what is the first thought that comes to mind?

2. Are there sins in your life that have or still hold you captive? If so, what are they?

3. How does the truth of Jesus Christ through salvation give freedom?

4. How have we as a society and individuals failed to see that God is the only truth we can trust in?

5. How does a lie, even a little one, affect your relationships?

6. Do you ever equate lying as one of the sins God despises the most? How does that affect your thoughts on lying?

7. How can you restore righteousness in your life from the lies you have told?

8. How can the TRUTH acronym help you remember the benefits of telling the truth?

   a. Spiritually
   b. Emotionally
   c. Physically

SESSION 6: GOD HAS TO MAKE ME HAPPY

I thank God for protecting me from what I thought I wanted,
and blessing me with what I didn't know I needed.

—unknown

What you want and what you get are often two different things. When I was in high school, I entered an architectural design competition. There were various phases to the competition that would be culminated in the final project to be publically displayed at the local county offices. I worked my hardest to develop the concept of the project, meticulously drafted the plans, researched the feasibility of materials, drew the artistic elevations, and finally built the model.

A lot of effort went into the project. However, I had placed so much effort into other phases that, when it came to building the model, I stayed up all night just hours before turning it in. I hurried through the process that would give the untrained eye the best view of my visionary for the project. I did not win the contest regardless of how good my drawings were.

I was sure I should have won the contest. I was the only high school student enrolled in the contest that was dual-enrolled in high school and a college architectural design program. However, the expectations for my work were higher because of that factor, not because I deserved the scholarship and recognition by positional default.

Our prayer lives are similar to that. We believe that God should answer all our prayers because we are believers. The idea that our faithfulness should constitute a requirement for God to make us happy is the same as the expectation that my educational position constituted a requirement for placing in the contest regardless of the poorly constructed model.

I hear it said all the time, "The Bible says that God will give me everything I want, so all my prayers should be answered." We believe that happiness is found in God telling us yes in every circumstance. The hard part is that we do not realize how damaging that really can be because He sees our future, and we do not.

When God doesn't answer our prayers, we become discouraged and feel as if God is not listening to us. When we are in emotional turmoil, we want God to come and give us joy that overcomes our emotional desires, thinking that if only God would answer my prayer for companionship, I would not be lonely anymore. If only God would take away my depression, I would not feel sad anymore.

We begin to believe our emotional state is because God does not answer our emotional wants and it is His fault we are suffering. Without blaming God, we always follow up with the thoughts of encouragement, "Well, in God's time, He will heal my emotional state." We rarely say, "God, in my emotional state, use me as a witness to others" or "God, while I am in this emotional storm, cover me with your protection so I can show others how you have brought me through." When we petition God, we are often petitioning Him for the wrong things.

Physically, we do the same thing. When I was a hospital chaplain, I had hundreds of people ask me to pray for what they wanted and not for God's will. They felt that God's will might not be what their will was, so they would ask God to heal their loved ones and then complain that prayer does not work because they simply prayed. Their prayers were not answered, but why would it be a surprise when you lift your petition to God and exert the thought and emotion of, "My will be done, God. Not yours, but mine"?

In the same respect, we pray for big houses, salaries, cars, and blessings because we think that asking God for the little stuff is too insignificant for Him to deal with, so "If we only had the big stuff in our lives, we would be able to attend to the little stuff ourselves." God will not give you the big stuff so you can remove Him from the little stuff.

We have to remember the little answered prayers in our lives are just as important as the big answered prayers. Within the little blessings we receive, do we have the opportunity to show good stewardship in order to receive the big blessings in life (Luke 16:10)? If we cannot recognize God in the little blessings, then we, in most cases, will take the big blessings for granted.

Taking God for granted is just as easy as feeling spiritually empty when the prayers are not answered. When we earnestly pray for something and we do not have the answered prayers, we might feel as if God is not listening to us, especially when people all around us are having their prayers answered in the specific way they have prayed for.

One day while ministering to some families in a pediatric cancer unit, I talked to two families. Ironically, both families were nurturing their child through the same difficult medical issue. The doctors were caring for the children with very similar treatment plans. Both families were devout in their prayer and dependence on God. I had very powerful conversations about the healing power of God. In fact, the two families spent a lot of time talking to each other about the difficulties of treatment and triumphs of battling their child's cancer. The difference was the outcome.

Regardless of how hard they prayed, how dedicated the doctors were in providing care, and how much both families loved their child, one of them passed away. Both families were devastated. One suffered from survivor's guilt, and the other suffered from overwhelming grief. They were so overwhelmed by the outcome of their prayers that neither family knew how to provide comfort for the other, not that either was responsible for doing so.

The family that lost their child was spiritually devastated. And rightly so. They began to question why they were the ones that God chose not to answer prayers for healing their child. They depended on the promise that, anything we ask of God, He would give it to them. They asked for the healing of their child, and that prayer, in their mind, was not answered.

Spiritual emptiness is common when we feel as if God has turned His back on us. "Doesn't God have to make us happy by answering our prayers?" The issue is that we believe that God owes us answered prayers the way we want them because we worship Him. It is similar to a child who becomes upset because his or her parent did not buy him or her a car for high school graduation. He or she thinks, "Well, you must not love me as you love everyone else. All my friends got one." Similarly, we say, "But

God, you answered all my friend's prayers. You must not love me like you love everyone else." The reality is that God loves us just the same, despite our unanswered prayers.

In return, we have one of two responses when we do not get what we want from God:

1. We try harder to get it. We think that maybe we did not pray hard enough or pray for the right things. Maybe we did not tithe enough or pay close enough attention in church. Whenever our prayers are not answered, we begin to evaluate our spiritual lives and push harder to be more spiritual. Additionally, we can begin thinking that God wanted us to do something to get the prayer answered. Believing this, we begin to take matters into our own hands. We work harder to get what we want, but we slowly push God out of the way to get there. Even as we continue to pray, we shift our prayers toward energy or perseverance to achieve our goals on our own. We begin to take on the attitude that God helps those who help themselves.

2. The other reaction is to become angry and begin blaming God for not answering our prayers. Just like a child who throws a temper tantrum, we blame God for not giving us what we wanted. We get upset and sometimes even walk away from God, the church, and everything that has to do with Christian spirituality. We believe, if God is not going to give us what we want, then we do not want anything to do with God. It's almost like, if you are not going to play the game by my rules, then I am going to take my ball and go home. The issue is, when we get angry with God, our vision for God is clouded, and we fail to see what God has in store for us instead. I knew someone who earnestly prayed for a promotion at work. She was adamant in getting the promotion and became so angry when passed over. Her anger seethed to the point that she determined prayer was useless. "If God is not going to hear and answer my prayer, then what's the use in asking God for anything?" she asked.

What she did not realize was that God had something better in store for her. A few months after she was turned down for promotion, she was offered a partnership in the organization. Where she wanted a promotion to senior team leader, God was able to bless her with something greater, but it was in God's timing that it would have been offered. Some growth took place, and she understood the way she handled the situation was more damaging to her spiritual life than helpful. At the beginning; however, she was angry.

Working harder to get our prayers answered as well as becoming angry is often fueled by the people we meet. The negative influences come from every direction in our lives. The secular world criticizes our devotion to pray or worship a God that many have never experienced. On the other hand, some Christians begin to attack our spiritual life and devotion toward God.

Job in the Old Testament is a perfect example of this (Job 22–24). As I have relayed the story before, Job was very sick. As he was laying in his ailments, he had some friends who came and visited him. For three days they sat with him quietly. Then the friends began to speak. They looked at Job and essentially accused him of sinning before God. They began to talk with him about repentance and said his healing would come when he repented whatever sin he had that God was punishing him for.

In the church today, we face similar issues. People will look at others and place judgment on them, telling them that prayers will not be answered because they have unrepented sin in their lives. While this could be true, it takes some real searching and understanding to make such an accusation. Too often the Christian community is too quick to judge others about sin if they do not know why someone's prayers are not being answered.

All over the world, there are people who are convinced they have horrible sin in their lives that prevent them from being able to have answered prayers. They have wants, dreams, and desires. They pray, hope, and have faith to become something more, not just for them but also for the kingdom of God. However, they are attacked from people who portray a higher class in the kingdom, but their attitude displays a lack of understanding.

When we see stories like this, it is easy to see the attack of misused

Christian theology. For some, the results of their behavior reflect their lot in life, but for many, their lot in life is not due to sin issue. This false theology only represents one attack, and faith surrounds the other attack.

People stand on the pedestal of a mustard seed to move mountains (Matt. 17:20; Luke 17:6). They tell people, if there is enough faith in their prayer, they can change any situation. I have seen people pray so hard and believe so much that their prayers will be answered that, when it does not happen, they will walk away from God completely. Some would say they did not have faith in the first place, but I would say they did not pray for God's will in the first place.

We can pray with the faith that moves mountains, and many people do, but if the prayer is outside God's will, the mountain might not move, but you will. We have to understand that mentoring people of God does not include attacking their faith, hope, or love, but guiding them toward an understanding of God's will.

This is not to say faith is not a vital part of prayer. It is to say that praying God's will and having faith in His direction for your life is even more vital. I have seen people lying dead on a hospital bed come back to life because of the faithful prayers of a parent, friend, or pastor. On the same note, the ones who are taken out of the hospital by the coroner were not because of a lack of faith from a praying parent, friend, or pastor.

As Christians, we cannot judge the faithfulness of other Christians in their personal prayer life. We can ensure they are praying with faith and within God's will, and for us to mentor them like that, it will build them up and help them understand how and why God answers prayers the way He does. We will look at that more later in this chapter by answering how we really address the myth that God is supposed to give us everything we ask for.

When we think about how our own Christian brothers and sisters criticize us, what expectation do we have for worldly advice? Worldly secularism has a major impact on our lives. We can look around at people who are of the world and become jealous of their possessions and positions in life. We ask ourselves where their faith is and why are they blessed but we are struggling to make ends meet. It would be easy for us to question God's will when we look at the world and question the things not of this world.

Too many people in worldly secularism tell us that faith in God must equate riches. They will ask how one can put his or her faith in a God that doesn't care about the Christian as much as the sinner. They use the belief that bad behavior warrants more attention and God wants us so much He would bless us more if He believes we are straying away just to save us. This social view is distorted and displays the thought process of privileged brats more than mature and dedicated believers.

They question our motives and assert that our lot in life is a direct result of God's love for us, but what we fail to realize is that our lot in life is not what matters, but our lot in eternity is what we place our hope in. Faith is the belief that our hope will be fulfilled in God's promise of eternity. We are not justified by our blessings here on earth, but by our righteousness in the kingdom of God.

If you were to answer someone with the response of being justified by faith and not tangible blessings when he or she says we as Christians serve a God who doesn't care, he or she might laugh or make fun. The reality though is that he or she would take another approach to discount the reality and truth of God. That would be to say that the God of Christians simply does not exist.

When I came into the military, most soldiers I worked with claimed some faith or belief system. Over the past twenty years, I have seen a slow shift. Adherence to some belief system went from a declaration of various faiths to no religious preference, and now an increasing number have declared agnostic or atheist as their preference. This shift in our society is just another attack on the sovereignty of God.

If we as believers are going to be able to understand that God does not have to make us happy and we have to pray in a way that fulfills God's calling in our lives, we have to understand the biblical justification people use to petition for their prayerful wants.

LOOKING AT THE CONTEXT

Asking for our heart's desires is not outside biblical promise. What is outside the biblical promise is what our heart's desire actually is. Often our heart's desire is outside of God's plan or will for our lives. Looking at the primary scriptures for God's promise to give us what we ask for, we can see the condition that God has for us. Nothing says He will just give it to us, but there are action and requirement on our parts.

ASK, SEARCH, KNOCK

Probably the most notable verses people use for the expectation of God granting our wishes like some magical genie is Matthew 7:7–12 and Luke 11:5–13. These two verses mirror each other when Jesus is teaching about the generosity and grace of God. Asking, searching, and knocking is not a matter of us being able to ask God for anything we want or take matters into our hands to search for the solutions to our problems. Even more, it is not a reason to go knocking on doors that do not need to be opened to us.

Both Matthew 7:7 and Luke 11:9 speak about asking, seeking, and knocking when it comes to God. We see this verse and automatically believe, if we ask for something, seek it, and knock on it, the blessings will flow in abundance. This is not always the case. We hold true to it because the following verse says, "Everyone who ask receives, and the one who searches finds, and the one who knocks the door will be opened" (Matt. 7:8).

If we break this down, we can see the expectations of God. "Keep asking, and it will be given to you" is the opening statement in verse 7, and the promise of everyone who asks receives in verse 8. When we read this, it naturally becomes apparent that whoever asks will receive because that is the promise in the Bible.

The promise in the Bible was not referring to asking God for material things. We have to pay attention to what we are asking for. In context of what Jesus was teaching, we can see He was talking about salvation. We are asking God to forgive us of our sins and asking for things that will draw us closer to God. Even more, if we are going to ask God for something, we have to make sure what we are asking for is exactly what God has intended for us. Without asking for what God has planned for us, we are simply asking for stuff outside of God's will.

Asking for things outside of God's will in our lives only draws us further away from God's plan for our lives. The further we get from asking for God's will, the more we try to take control of what happens to us. When we want something so bad that we leave God on the wayside and strive to obtain it ourselves, we lose the covering of God in everything we do. Ultimately we begin to search for things on our own, and we justify the independent search as a mandate based in the next section of the verse.

"Keep searching, and you will find" is the next promise. Once again, in verse 8, it says, "The one who searches finds." Our search is never ending. It is something we have to find, whether it be the answers to difficult questions or the act to obtain what we ask for. Often we spend our entire lives searching without finding the answers or obtaining the goal.

Asking ourselves what our purpose is or why things happen the way they do will always leave people searching for something more. So often, when we go on a search, we begin looking for things of this world. We search for satisfaction of our own personal desires rather than the satisfaction of our spiritual desires. It is our responsibility to begin searching for spiritual desires in life rather than everything the world has to offer.

Asking and seeking will lead to expectation. When we get into our heads that we want something, we expect that someday we would get it. It might be that we need to earn enough money for it or we will extend credit to obtain it. No matter what the cost is, we will do what we can to have it. If you truly look around at the people you associate with that seem to have everything, ask yourself how they got it all. Are they in debt so much they have no residual funds, or are they blessed?

When we see the people who are in debt to the point they pay bills with each paycheck instead of having cash on hand, you will see people who have taken things into their own hands. These people have strayed away from God's will and timing in order to obtain what they want in life outside of God's will. We cannot live our lives paying credit card bills because we lacked the faith that God would provide for our needs as He has promised. This would mean that we believe we needed it more than God knew we didn't need.

In the same respect, there are people who have been blessed in great abundance. Many of them have waited, prayed, and constantly knocked on the door of opportunity until it opened. When we see the people who might not have everything, we usually see people who also do not have mounds of debt. Often, but not always, it is because they remained in line with what God's will was for their life, and the doors were opened.

This leads to knocking. The last promise is that if we keep knocking, the door would be opened to us (Matt. 7:7). Later in verse 8, it says, "To the one who knocks, the door will be opened." When I hear this in relation to the people getting what they want from God, it reminds me of the popular analogy used in many churches. "Well, God opened that door for me, and He shut the others."

There is nothing wrong with that if God truly opened the door for you but if you are the type of person that asks God and you bust down the door when you do not get what you want, that is not considered an open door. This means you are holding true to the mantra that "God helps those who help themselves." You once again have moved outside the will of God and took what you wanted before God could bless you with what you needed.

We have to realize that some doors are easier to break down than others are. This is not because God makes weak doors. It's because Satan makes weak doors. The doors we can bust down are ones that Satan puts in our way to make us move away from the ones God intends to open for us. When we knock at the door that we know God is behind, He will open it for us, and He will let us pass through.

Recently I was looking back at journal entries from when I was praying about going into ministry. I can see the desire of my heart and the prayers asking God to confirm the ministry, all seeking wisdom and discernment in the decision. Then I see where I broke down a door in ministry that caused a major setback. I knew God had called me to ministry, I knew the direction He wanted me to move, and I wanted it right then. I am not the only one who has made this mistake. Tons of people jump the gun to serve God or get their prayers answered, only to be turned off and turned away from God because it did not happen the way they imagined it would.

I was so frustrated that I wanted to leave ministry all together. I was angry because I thought, if God really called me to it, then why do I have to wait for it to happen? What I did not realize is that we have to wait for the door to be opened. We cannot just barge in on God's plan for us. God is preparing everything and setting everything in place for when He opens the door.

It is like cleaning the house before company arrives. You want everything in place, so when your guests come in, they see the beauty, not the family cleaning. When God opens the door, we get to see the blessing, not everything that went into the blessing. If we bust down the door, we might interrupt the preparation that God is making for us, and the blessing might not be as beautiful as God intended it to be.

This leads to a word that some translations have and others do not, the word "keep." The verses in Matthew and Luke say to keep asking, seeking, and knocking. This does not mean we nag God for what we want. It means we have to be patient for God to prepare what He has for us. When we remain consistent in the promises of God, He remains consistent in fulfilling these promises. We have to remember to be steadfast in our hope because, if we are not steadfast in our hope, we will take matters in our own hands. Being steadfast means going through the process to learn and prepare for what God has in store for us, even if it does take a long time to get.

We have to keep doing the things laid out in this verse, right in line with God's plan. Doing so will allow us to keep God first in our lives. When He is number one, we will cling to the promises that we do not have to search for what we ask for, search for the answers, or break doors down to get it because God will provide in His time and within His will for our lives.

Sometimes the issue is not that we are asking God for something, but what we are asking God for. God's only intention is to give us the best blessings and gifts. In His infinite wisdom, He will give us what is best according to our calling. Jesus paints this picture when He compares the gifts of an earthly father (Matt. 7:9–11; Luke 11:11–13).

A father's love for his family is incomparable. A true father will always provide for his family. They will attempt to give the best of what they have for their children. Giving the best is not because gifts and supplying needs is the way to show love, but it's because this is an act of love toward their family. Jesus takes this understanding of masculine culture and relates it to God's love for His people. Just as a father only hopes to give the best of what he has to offer his family, God desires to give the best of what He has to offer to us. No earthly father would give his child stones, snakes, or scorpions when the family needs bread, fish, or eggs. This is a stark contrast of what God has to offer His people.

When Jesus gives this list, note the two differences. One represents the sustainment of life, while the others are tools used to bring death, pain, and suffering. No father wants to supply his child with death and suffering, and if that were the case, then why would the heavenly Father desire that for His children? Even those who are evil fathers desire to give the best gifts to their children deep down inside.

Some would beg to differ on that thought. With a world that is plagued with child abuse and corruption, the thought of an evil father giving his children the best is far-fetched. Christ was not referring to the evils of child abuse and corruption, but he was describing the evils of sin. Every one of us is a sinner, and because of his, we do not always give our children what is best for them.

As parents, we have to strive to bring life to our children through the giving of good gifts, just as Christ strives to bring us the best gifts, the ones that bring spiritual, emotional, and physical life. However, in the midst of our sin, we do not always make the best decisions for our children, but that does not mean we do not want the best for our children.

The parent who falls to sin every day, which is all of us, does not desire the worst for his or her child. Jesus makes this comparison because, in our imperfection, we want the best for our child so we can understand God only wants the best for us in His perfection. In the midst of our sin, we will often see worldly desire over what the truly good gifts are.

The good gifts bring sustainment of life, and through those gifts, we understand how God hungers to only give us His best blessings. We, however, are like the child in the store who asks for everything we see despite how good it is for us.

If you walk through any store today, you will see two types of parents. The first type has no issue telling his or her child no; the second is afraid to tell his or her child no. Some would argue they are giving their child everything they never had. I would argue they are spoiling their child to the point of arrogance and entitlement. So many people will give their children gifts that are not the best for them. Some would bring spiritual, emotional, and physical death.

In order to receive the good gifts of life, we have to be in line with what God has planned for our lives. Our prayer lives cannot resemble the child in the store but must look like someone who is discerning and wise. Yes, there will be times we ask for something that we really want, but God is going to know what the best gift is for us, and He will bless us accordingly. We have to remember that sometimes God chooses not to answer our prayer because He desires the best for us, not because He just does not care.

We are not entitled to answer prayer for everything, but we are blessed with the very best gifts for who God wants us to be. Our society today says we should be entitled to everything because the person next to us has it, but it never looks at the individualism that God is molding us to be. When we pray, we should be asking that God bless us with the best of what He has for us in our lives. To receive truly good gifts from God, align your desires with God.

As we know, God does not just give us what we are asking for, but sometimes when we are asking for something good, something we feel like we are in line with God on, we still do not get it. The passage in Matthew 7 has a statement that Luke does not: "Whatever you want others to do for you, do also the same for them" (Matt. 7:12).

This is a conditional promise. To expect good gifts from God but not expect to share your blessings with others is selfish. This is in line with many of Christ's teachings. Simply put, this is the love of God manifested in our actions. If we expect the blessings of God, we have to be willing to bless others.

God does not give us the good gifts so we can selfishly improve our lot in the kingdom of heaven, but so we can use those gifts to minister to others through our testimony, devotion, and blessing the lives of others. What good is a blessing if you cannot use it to bless others?

This concept goes beyond treating others the way you want to be treated. It transcends the thought that if you are nice to others, others will be nice to you, but it crosses into the thought that you become the blessing for others because God has given you that ability.

We have to take what God has given us and learn how to turn it into a blessing for others. This could be simply tithing appropriately on Sunday mornings or using a skill to provide for a need in your community or church. Paramount to this thought is that you are willing to serve God through giving of yourself because God equipped you with the ability to bless them.

The goal is to bring life to others in need because God has brought life to you. The greatest blessing this could be is through sharing the gospel message. After all, the greatest blessing in any Christian's life is the grace found in salvation. Others do not know what salvation is. They do not know what it is like to have every sin and burden lifted off their shoulders because the greatest gift was Christ who died for their sins. We share this gift through word and deed because people will not know what the good gift of salvation is without us showing them who Jesus is and telling them what he did for us.

In Jesus's Name, Let It Be So

The second verse I hear people quoting is John 14:13–14, "Whatever you ask in My name, I will do it so that the Father may be glorified in the Son. If you ask Me anything in My name, I will do it." Some translations omit verse 14, but verse 13 is similar in the fact that Christ asserts asking in his name to receive anything.

As a result, people will consistently end their prayers with the statement "In Jesus's name." When we hear this statement, we are asking in the name of Christ, as He has directed, but we have to understand it is not who we are asking for in that moment. What we are asking for makes the difference.

We have to remember that prayer is a petition to God for our heart's desire. Praying in Jesus's name is to commit that petition to God through Jesus Christ. It is not a way to sway God's direction for our lives. If we were to ask God to kill all our enemies, it might not be a prayer to be answered. The issue we always face, as I have written above, is that we must not ask God to grant us things outside His will. If we ask God for things outside His will, we will find ourselves falling short.

Jesus points out two important requirements that people must understand in order to grasp the concept of praying in Jesus's name. It is not just a pithy ending to a prayer, but it's something that must be meditated on, believed, and stated with the right intention. First, Jesus says at the end of verse 13, "So the Father may be glorified in the Son." Verse 14 continues with the second requirement that is also found at the beginning of verse 13, and that is to ask in Jesus's name.

Since verse 14 is not in some translations, I want to concentrate on verse 13. I believe the same points can be made through this verse, and verse 14 only adds emphasis to the thought of asking in Jesus's name. There is no mystery to the beginning of verse 13, Jesus says, "Whatever you ask in My name, I will do it." As simple and straightforward as it could be, that is not the end of the statement because he continues, "So that the Father may be glorified in the Son." Here is the kicker for all of us to remember. In the midst of this, we can ask in Jesus's name all we want, but if the intention is not so God is glorified, we have failed to ask in the right heart.

So many people leave this powerful statement out of their thought processes in prayer. Oftentimes we pray for things in our lives for our own benefit and glory. I want to win the lottery. I wish I had that new car. I want to be brought out of the storm I am facing in life. The answer is very simple. We do not want these things so God can be glorified. We want them so we can be comfortable.

Many of our prayers in life today are for our comfort and protection, not for God's grace and glory. When we pray for things, we pray with selfish intention. I remember hearing someone pray, and if someone stood up against him, he would pray that God's wrath would fall upon him or her. He honestly believed, if he asked for God's wrath in Jesus's name, it would happen. It was not for God to be glorified. It was because he did not like the person and wanted to see him or her destroyed.

Glorifying God as a result of our petitions is the part of being a Christian that asserts surrendering our wants and desires and inspires us to pick up our cross and follow Christ (Matt. 16:24–26). This means that we, as Paul says, die to ourselves every day (1 Cor. 15:31). There are plenty of things we want, and in some cases, we feel we should have because of our hard work, but there are many times we will fall short of those desires because our intention is not to glorify God in anything we do.

If we want our prayers to be answered, we have to give attention to those who will be lifted up in them. Is it for us to determine what should be given? Do we have the right to demand prominence on this earth because of our position in heaven? By no means do we only have the right and awesome responsibility to give our lives and our every being to loving God and our neighbors. We have to be willing to sacrifice ourselves and everything we want so glory abounds in the kingdom.

Our motivation for prayer cannot be what we want for ourselves, which is like a child in the grocery store who throws a temper tantrum because he did not get the kind of cereal he wanted. As believers, we need to stop expecting that God will give us everything we want just to make us happy and be ready to receive exactly what God wants to give us in order to prepare us for His future blessings.

For God to prepare us, it might mean we have to go through the storm, all the way through the storm. Facing the trials in life is not punishment. It is where God has placed us in His sovereignty for His glory. If your place in life right now is in the midst of trials, then He has an intention, and He will protect you through the storm and bring you through it.

When you are asking for something in Jesus's name, remember the intention you are asking for. God did not say, "Anytime you throw a temper tantrum in my name, I will give you what you want." He said, "If you ask anything in my name, I will give it to you so God many be glorified."

We have to change our prayer focus that, when we do pray in the name of Jesus, we are receiving the blessing because of who we want to receive the glory. Essentially God has our treasures stored in heaven, not on this earth, but if we want to be rich on earth, we have to understand that it is like receiving our inheritance before it is time. Nothing says God should give us everything we want. It says He will give us everything we ask for in order to glorify His name.

What We Should Use Instead

I could end this chapter with the thoughts from John 14, but I believe it is important to break down this concept in an understanding of why our prayers might not be answered. The overarching concept is designed around who should receive the glory, but what about the times we pray for things we intend for God's glory and they do not come to pass?

Some would say, in that instance, God did not need to be glorified in that area. Maybe even God knew the true intention of your heart in the midst of that prayer. However, John gives the hint for effective prayer in 1 John 5:14–15, This passage is the formula that is necessary to be effective when asking God for something. The first statement that John makes is that we have to ask according to God's will (1 John 5:14b), but more when we do this, God will hear us.

John's understanding of effective prayer will help us understand why our prayers fall short. When people earnestly believe in what they pray, they believe they are speaking the request into existence. This means they have the faith that what they are saying will happen. I wish this worked every time because my football teams would win every weekend and fantasy football would be easy for me. There are people who speak things into existence because they know it is to glorify God, and many of these requests come to pass. However, there are people who speak things into existence, and the opposite happens.

Is it because they lack the faith to believe it will happen? I remember one Sunday when I was on a prayer team at a local church. I stood at the front of the sanctuary, waiting for someone to come and ask for prayer. As I stood there, I could see a man who suffered from a terminal illness coming toward me. I thought to myself, *Dear God, don't let this man come to me. There is no way my prayer for healing will help him.*

Sure enough, he walked up to me and said, "Ryan, God told me to have you pray for my healing, so here I am."

This was a huge step, and I thought there was no way I would be able to say a prayer that would provide healing for this man. The issue was not that my prayer would provide healing, but I needed to step out in the faith that God would hear my prayer, just as much as the man who asked for prayer stepped out of his seat and walked up to me because he felt the prompting of the Holy Spirit for me specifically to pray for him. I prayed for him, but not with the confidence that I should have. I prayed what I thought I should pray, and honestly, when I look back on it, it was a faithless prayer.

Did God answer my prayer? I don't know, but I do know that he was more faithful than I was in that prayer. My vision was whether my prayer could provide healing when it should have been because of this man's faithfulness. God will be faithful, and so should I.

There was a lot to be learned in my arrogance. First, my prayers were not for my glory, but God's. Second, I needed to step out in faith and believe what God had empowered me to do in His name (John 14:12). Finally, I needed to change my thought process on intercessory prayer. We have to remember that our prayers do not move God toward a decision on an issue. Our prayers show God the faithfulness needed that we might ask Him for anything despite ourselves.

WHY GOD DOES NOT ANSWER OUR PRAYERS

Through that experience, I developed four primary reasons that God does not answer prayer. The unfortunate part is that most of us have fallen victim to one or all of these in our lives. I have seen many of them take place in churches, small groups, and even personal prayer lives everywhere.

1. **We don't believe God can answer them**. We have to remember that God will answer our prayers because He answered Jesus's

prayers. In John 14:12, we can see where Christ instructs the disciples that they are able to do great works because He is going to God. We have to believe that God will answer our prayers because He is limitless in His desires for our lives. His limitless is something we cannot fathom; therefore, we become victims of our perception of possibility. We often believe in the things that we can see or prove the possibility of existing. Whether we like science or not, we often operate in a process of scientific method that limits the holy. Through a process of deduction, we make determination of the possibility that something can actually happen. When it does happen outside our understanding, we call it an anomaly, not a miracle. In order for us to see answered prayers, we have to believe our prayers can be answered. This is a matter of faith—true, honest, childlike faith. This is faith that bypasses an understanding of what could feasibly happen to one who dreams the possibility that anything can happen in the hands of God. If we want our prayers answered, we have to believe that God can answer them.

2. **We have the wrong motives**. Their motives are directed by personal selfishness instead of desire to serve God. James writes to the church, "You ask and don't receive because you ask with wrong motives, so that you may spend it on your evil desires" (James 4:3). James was talking about the evil desires of people who have prideful intention for their lives. When we pray in a way that focuses on our desire to be rich or famous or increase our status, we are praying with a prideful heart. As some of the previous stories relate, pride will not allow our prayers to be answered because God will not receive the credit for our triumphs. Tons of examples in the Bible speak to people who depended on God and then fell short because they believed it was they were able to succeed through their strength and power. When we overcome insurmountable odds with unknown success, we can chalk it up to skill, or we can recognize that God is the giver of all blessing. There is nothing in our lives that we can solely take credit for because help comes from every direction. If we want our prayers to be answered, we have to align ourselves with God's will and be willing to give Him credit for our accomplishments.

3. **We have unconfessed sin in our lives.** Unconfessed sin is difficult because it is the first question we ask when prayers are not answered. Isaiah writes about this when he lets the Israelites know their prayers are not answered because of sin in their lives (Isa. 59:1–2). The issue we have to understand is that God does not withhold prayer requests because of sin issues in one's life. If this were the case, no one would have an answered prayer because everyone has sin, and almost everyone I know has unconfessed sin in his or her life (Rom. 3:23). While every believer should bring his or her wrongdoings to the cross, some of us have so much in our lives that we cannot bring it all. However, we can ask God to search our hearts and make us clean according to His glory in heaven. This is the key to unconfessed sin, that the Holy Spirit would make us clean, not that we confess everything we have ever done wrong in our lives. Through Christ, we are brought into glory, not through a list of wrongdoings but the admittance of our sinful lives. This glory allows the Holy Spirit to come into our lives and wipe us clean of all wrongdoing. When we do not have answered prayer because of unconfessed sin, it is because we do not trust in the Holy Spirit to make us clean. If we do not have faith that we can be sanctified through the grace of the Holy Spirit, how can we say we have faith that our prayers will be answered? The key is not that we have unconfessed sin in our lives as much as we do not have the faith to turn toward God to forgive our sinfulness. Therefore, we lack faith in the Holy Spirit to answer our prayers. It is a matter of dependence on God for everything in our lives, from making us clean to answering our prayers.

4. **We have established idols that get between God and us**. Idolatrous behavior is the very thing that takes us away from God. When we enter into idolatrous relationships, we are not yanked from the grasp of God, but we slowly fade away from Him. When we put the obstacles of this world in between God and us, we have failed to make God our priority. In this case, why should God consider our petitions before Him (Ezek. 14:3)? It almost seems crazy to think that God might not answer our prayers, especially when the Bible tells us that God bestows His blessings upon the

wicked as much as the righteous (Matt. 5:45). If this is the case, we know He hears all the prayers of His people and answers those prayers according to His will. However, when your will and His conflict with each other, then prayers are not answered in the way we want them to. Ezekiel was describing this issue in the passage mentioned above. The people had allowed idols to get between them and God, and as a result, they felt God was no longer faithful to their needs. In your prayer life, self-examination is key. This will help identify the things that have gotten between you and God and can inhibit your relationship with Him. By simply asking God to identify the idols in your life and to give you strength when removing them, you are better equipped to make the changes that will align your prayer request with God's will. Never for a moment think that God would give you something that would draw you further away from Him. We have to remember that God's desire is to draw us closer to Him, not push us further away. For this reason, He will never answer a prayer that He knows will cause us to fall deeper into idolatrous behaviors. Even when our words say we will glorify Him if we only had something, God knows the inner workings of our heart, sometimes the deepest parts of our heart that we do not even know about. In those places, God identifies the idols and can see how it will draw us away from Him.

Five Ways God Answers Our Prayers

When we do not get the answer that we are looking for, we believe that God did not answer us. Oftentimes we do not realize is that God answers all our prayers. This becomes an issue because we find happiness in getting what we want from God. Without fail, we regularly fall short of discerning God's will for our lives. We have to understand that God will answer our prayers in different ways. Not all of them are the ways we want.

Looking at the five ways God will answer our prayer, we can see, regardless the answer, God extends passion and wisdom in each of them. Instead of looking for God as the sugar daddy that should give us everything we want, we should look toward God as the wise Father who guides us out of self-destruction.

We have to remember that God is our creator and sustainer, not someone who had no selection or input in our lives, but someone who molded us in detail for exactly who we were to be in His kingdom. Therefore, when God tells us no within our petitions to Him, we have to trust that He knows us better than ourselves because He built us. Within God's sovereignty, we see the following five answers when we lift our petitions to God:

- No, it's not my will because I love you too much.
- Yes, but you're not ready yet. It will happen in my timing.
- Yes, but not exactly how you asked for it. I tweaked it just for you.
- Yes, but the blessing will be greater than you ever expected.
- Yes, I am glad you finally sought me for this need.

The five ways God answers our prayers gives us no doubt that God loves you and me, more than we will ever know.

FOUR-POINT PRAYER AND MEDITATION

Until this point, we focused on how God will receive our prayers, but when I talk with people about prayer, they often do not know how to pray. In many cases, our prayer lives are filled with bouts of talking at God, but rarely do they include talking with God. For someone to truly hear the voice of God in the things he or she does, we have to be ready to hear His voice. It is not always a booming exclamation of God's direction for our lives. When it is a soft whisper, we often feel God only listens, so we take matters in our own hands and move on.

Remember that God desires relationship with us, and relationship requires two-way communication. If there is not two-way communication, how can we expect God to give us answer? As a result, we should be able to enter into our time with God in a way that will create an environment that builds relationship, not continue to foster a relationship that results in talking at God instead of talking with Him.

Regardless of the time we set aside to spend with God, we should divide our time into quarters. No time with God should be entered into haphazardly, but should be entered with reverence and respect for who

God is in our lives. The below method was developed so that, as we enter into our time with God, we are able to communicate and build a relationship with Him.

The first quarter of our time with God should be spent preparing our hearts and removing all the obstacles that could draw our attention from Him. Many people will go into their quiet time with God by playing soft music. We do not realize that our quiet time is not quiet if we are entering into a sacred space playing music, having the television in the background, or even trying to pray in a public place where people are talking. Quiet time means just that. Go somewhere quiet, and prepare your heart to spend time with God.

Preparing your heart to spend time with God also means that you clear your mind from all the distractions that might take away from focusing on whom you are spending time with. There are times we get ready to pray, and we end up making our to-do list for the day, wonder where or what we are having for lunch, or deal with the stressors of the day that have nothing to do with our prayers.

In order for us to have an impactful prayer time, we have to be ready to give God our attention. We must be prepared to spend time with God and only Him. No matter the amount of time, whether it is one minute or ninety, preparing our heart in the first quarter of the time will prepare us to devote our time to God.

Prayer is important, and the next quarter of the time should be spent petitioning God. This can be any way you want to lift your praises, concerns, or needs to God. I have always been taught that praising God should be the first thing that comes out of your mouth when you approach Him. There are many reasons for this thought, but the primary motive is that nothing happens in our lives without the mercy and grace of God. For this reason, we should give Him honor, glory, and praise. I know some people who feel praising God or giving praise reports is boastful, so they do not do it. But when your praise is to glorify God instead of brag about what you have received, there is nothing boastful about praise.

The second thing I have been taught about prayer is to lift your concerns to God. These are prayers for the people around you: friends, enemies, and family. Remember that it is always easy to pray for your friends and family, but praying for your enemies is never easy. Pastorally,

I have heard stories of those who prayed for Islamic extremists and were chastised because of it. In the same respect, as I wrote above, I knew a pastor who prayed for his enemies by asking God to destroy them. When we pray for our enemies, we have to remember that we are asking God to deal with their heart, to allow His grace to fall on them and for them to find and know His unconditional love.

Finally we pray for our needs. These are things that we want and should not be considered selfish desires. So many people feel the only prayer request they should give is for their friends and families, but when they give their own prayer requests, they withhold because they are afraid that someone might hold it against them or they are being selfish. In fact, some believe their prayers are too insignificant to lift to God compared to prayers for cancer, grief, or desperate job searches. What we don't realize is that we should cast all our cares upon Jesus (Ps. 55:22; 1 Peter 5:7).

God never instructed us to cast only the major life events on Him, but everything should be lifted to God. When we pray for our needs, never think something is too insignificant to lift toward God. Sometimes the most insignificant things in our lives will show how much He loves us because an answered prayer for something insignificant shows that God cares about the little details as much as He does for the big events in our lives.

The third quarter of the time should be in the stillness of the moment. This is the hard part for so many people. Often our thoughts are geared toward what we want, and we leave out the time to be still and know (Ps. 46:10). It is in this stillness that we wait upon the Lord.

We are not waiting for God to instantly answer our prayers, but for Him to speak into our lives. He will give us wisdom (James 1:5) and direction (Ps. 32:8), and He will speak into our lives in a way we can hear in the quietness of our time with Him.

We have a hard time hearing God because of the loudness of life. Our lives are so busy that we fill every second with calendar events and programs. And even when we have down-time, we search for something to do. It is difficult to hear God when there is so much noise in our lives. However, when we sit quietly and wait upon the Lord, the noise of life is canceled out, and the sound of His voice can be heard.

It is important to remember in this step that it takes practice to sit and wait upon the Lord. It is not natural for us to sit in quiet stillness anymore. In fact, it is sometimes uncomfortable to sit quietly. This is a concept that many people are not able to comprehend because they are afraid of losing control in the quietness. Losing control in the quietness of God's presence is giving God control to speak into your life. Just do not expect to hear God speak into your life right away because, for many Christians, His voice is not recognizable just yet. This is because it has been so long since they actually heard God's voice speak into their lives.

Finally, take the last moments of your time to reconnect and reflect. This means you might be able to turn on some soft music or begin thinking about what happened in your prayer time. This is an opportunity for you to journal the experience you had. No matter how you reconnect with life around you or reflect on your time with God, it is important to take this step. If you had an especially moving time with God in prayer and meditation, just jumping up and going about your business will leave you in a state of shock. This feeling makes you feel cloudy in the head, as if you just woke up from a nap.

The best example of this would be going on a wonderful date. If you think about the best date you have ever been on and how you reflected on that date and wanted nothing more than to see the person again, then you will be able to understand the four-point prayer process. The goal is to spend that amount of time with God to the point where you cannot wait to be with Him again. Eventually the time we spend with God will increase, and the process will become natural.

CHAPTER 5

SELF-REFLECTION OR SMALL GROUP DISCUSSION QUESTIONS

1. What are ways you have been discouraged by others (other Christians, coworkers, family, friends, and so forth) when your prayers did not seem to be answered?

2. How does the word "keep" (Matt. 7:7; Luke 11:9) change your perspective on patience and perseverance when asking God for something in prayer?

3. Not all gifts are good for us despite how much we want them. Knowing what good gifts are, how is your perspective changed when asking God for something?

4. How have you used your blessings to bless others?

5. Does your prayer life reflect intention to glorify God?

6. What stumbling blocks in your life get in the way of recognizing how God answers your prayers?

7. How do you feel your prayers align with the will of God in your life?

8. Of the five ways God answers prayers in our lives, how do you feel God answers most of your prayers?

9. In the four-point prayer process, what point do you most commonly leave out?

10. After reading this chapter, how has your understanding of God's answered prayers changed? Does He have to make you happy, or does His love for you supersede spoiling you?

SESSION 7: IT'S ALL GOOD

The world can create trouble in peace, but God can create peace in trouble.

—Thomas Watson

I have had some really bad things happen to me in life. There are instances where I don't feel like I will every make it through the issue. The fog of distress impairs my ability to see the positive in a situation. Even more, I do not see how I can get out of it. Regardless, I have made it past my mistakes and through the trials. Each of those times, God has allowed me to learn from the experience.

I know I am not much different from other people. I have counseled people for years who are in the fog of life's battles. Each of these people believe he or she is facing insurmountable odds that will prevent him or her from ever recovering in life. When they face these odds and come to me, one of the biggest complaints is that people always tell them that God will use their situation for good. They are encouraged with the amount of good that will come out of the situation without the hope of making it through.

This is very common across the world today. Something terrible happens. There is a major life-changing event that so many people cannot see their way out of. Inevitably someone will tell them that God will use their life trauma for good. What we do not realize is that, in the midst of the storm, most people are trying to figure out how to get out of the rain, not how God will be glorified in the situation.

Most commonly this is seeing in the physical aspect. People who lose loved ones or children often do not want to hear that God will use the situation for His glory in the midst of their trial. The mother of a child who was killed in a drive-by shooting or was the victim of a drunk driving accident does not immediately think, "God will use this for His glory." The only thing they are going to be thinking about is how to get through the situation and why something like this even happened.

God's glory comes out later at a time when the person has come to terms with the situation. It happens when this individual reaches a point in his or her life where he or she can fathom what has happened and determine on his or her own that he or she would never want someone else to go through the same event. This idea produces wonderful public service programs, dynamic speakers, and inspiring stories that draw people closer to God.

These speakers and programs appeal to the emotion in a way that will help others become inspired and motivated to live a better life, although for those who are in emotional storms it is hard to see how God can use something for His glory. As a military chaplain, I can see this regularly with those suffering from post-traumatic stress disorder. These people have images, events, and memories imprinted on their lives. Those suffering from emotional trauma have things that no one will ever be able to take away, yet they are expected to function in a social setting that does not normally pose those same threats.

This also does not dispel the emotional issues caused by stress, depression, and other emotionally difficult situations. People who are affected by emotional events or situations in their lives face insurmountable odds because they are often discouraged by the struggles they face every day. For people to say God can use their emotional pain for His glory is difficult to believe because most people who experience life-debilitating emotional strife cannot see beyond the midst of their struggles.

This emotional blindness prevents people from seeing God in their everyday life. Imagine experiencing life without the thought, sight, and dependence on God because you are physically and emotionally not able to see Him. This could be especially difficult if you have experienced God in the past. It would be like a person who loses his or her sight after being able to enjoy the wonders and beauty of the world. He or she knows what it is like to see and, in many cases, desire to see again, but cannot because of his or her circumstance.

For people in the midst of emotional and spiritual trauma, it is difficult for them to see or savor God in their life, regardless of God's presence. It is not because they do not want more of God or to get their way out of the difficult situation, but they can't see their way out.

When people are in the midst of spiritual strife, it is arrogant for others to believe they can get them to snap out of it by telling them God will make their situation better or use their trauma for His glory. I know it is the desire of all believers to give hope in the midst of hopelessness. It is not a statement that will give them hope, but the ability for them to experience God in the midst of their trauma will provide hope. We have to remember their lives are turned upside down and chaos surrounds them. In most cases, people who face insurmountable trials and tribulations in life desire peace. The challenge as a believer is guiding them to a place where they can experience that peace.

Looking at the Context

This statement does not come in some random attempt to encourage people. The theology comes from Genesis 50:20 and Romans 8:28. Both verses reflect the belief that everything works together for good. In the Genesis passage, Joseph finds restoration in relationship with his brothers and makes the statement that their actions, though indented for evil, have been made good because his place in the world has saved many people (Gen. 50:20). As well, in Romans, Paul instructs the Roman people, "All things work together for the good of those who love God" (Rom. 8:28).

There is truth in this statement because God does make everything work for the good of all people. The statement is misused in our timing and delivery. When people are in the middle of trying to figure everything out, forcing them to think about how God is going to use the situation does not help. The best time to do that is when they have come to terms with the situation.

This does not mean we don't point them toward God. It means we point them toward God in a way that brings peace and comfort. A level of fear is involved in the midst of our trials that we often can't see past. Looking at the interaction between Joseph's brothers and him, you can see their fear in the situation (Gen. 50:15–18).

THREE CHARACTERISTICS OF FEAR IN TRIALS

Three characteristics present themselves when we allow fear to consume us after we have wronged someone. The brothers display all three of these characteristics in rapid succession. First, it is easy to worry about grudges that take away from forgiveness and focuses on revenge as the reaction to wrongdoings (Gen. 50:15). The social norm we see today focuses on how people have wronged us, and when we know we have wronged another person, the first thought is how they might get even. This is why we hear "what comes around goes around" more than "I'm sorry."

Joseph's brothers were no different. They were worried about his positional ability to retaliate against them. Therefore, they took the next step toward preventing retaliation. They lied to him (Gen. 50:16). This is a perfect example of a string of lies covered by more lies in order to avoid getting in trouble.

When we are fearful that something bad might happen to us or we think we might be able to get out of a life trial quicker, it is easy for us to make up a lie. There are many reasons why we lie (see chapter 4). Regardless, lying to get through a trial or to cover guilt only leads to more stress in the situation.

Joseph's brothers formatted a message that his father had died and his dying wish was that Joseph would forgive his brothers. In verse 17, Joseph breaks down in great distress over the message. Some would say because he did not want to forgive his brother, but the following verses will dispel that notion. Before we get to those verses, Genesis 15:18 shows the continual attempt to cover up a situation. It appears that Joseph's brothers use reverse psychology on him to test the waters. They bow down and tell Joseph they are his servants.

Knowing you should be punished for your actions and knowing the person you wronged has the power to retaliate will cause us to accept defeat and attempt to submit to some level of punishment. I see it with my children all the time when they are not sure what decision or direction I might take with discipline so they submit to a punishment that seems harsh but is not the worst that could happen. This is simply testing the waters.

My children will admit the wrongdoing and suggest a punishment, and it is up to me to make the decision if I am going to grant forgiveness, accept their terms for punishment, or be stricter. Testing the water means they will try to gauge which direction I will go with my punishment and try to negotiate the terms of discipline. Looking at this passage, I believe Joseph was being challenged with the same predicament when his brothers bowed before him and said they would be his servants (Gen. 15:18).

Here we can see where God can make even the worst of situations good. Joseph's band of jealous brothers was trying to change their lot in life. They deserved a greater punishment, only protected by their father in his life and submitted to fearful deceit in their father's death.

When people are going through trials in their lives, they are looking for confidence. They want confidence to know God will carry them through the storm, and though they might come out with bumps and bruises, they will survive the trials. This part makes Joseph's story so powerful. We can look at it from a perspective that Joseph extended forgiveness even when he did not have to. In fact, this story can show the wonderful graces that can be extended to others in the midst of transgressions. All of us can learn a lesson in forgiveness from this entire passage.

However, in the midst of Joseph's response, we find the truth of God making everything good. We can see where the trials Joseph went through, and the trials we might go through are right where God has placed us in his perfect will and sovereign design (Gen. 50:19–20).

There is a saying, "You were in the wrong place at the wrong time." This is to say that you were not where you needed to be and something bad happened. You might have been drawn into the situation in a way that makes you suspect to something or even accused of wrongdoing because of your proximity. Some people even believe that our fate or destiny causes us to be part of certain events in life because of little mishaps in our lives that delay or quicken our usual routine.

This is not always negative either. Some people believe they have avoided serious accidents because they lost their keys on the way in to work or because the coffee shop was unusually busy that day. Many of these stories came out of the September 11 attacks. A lot of people were praising God for the delay, but when they were in the midst of the delay, it was most likely a huge frustration. An upset routine in the normal day is frustrating and common to all people.

However, few people will look at the incident as God's sovereign design. The reality is that we have a hard time seeing anyone being in the towers or on a plane, dying that kind of death, and believe it is part of God's plan. Some may never find peace in the aftermath of that event or the years of war that followed. Regardless, we have to have confidence that, somewhere in the midst of all that tragedy, God had an ultimate plan that has to play out.

Believing in God's sovereign design means He has ordained every breath and situation we are in (1 Thess. 5:18). Nothing happens outside the authority of God, and in the midst of this, God's will is accomplished. This is a hard concept to comprehend because our trials seem as if God does not care about the suffering of the world.

The sovereignty of God enforces the thinking that these evils have to happen in order for God to pave the way to His kingdom, a place where those who have faith and belief in Him might find ultimate peace. Without the sovereignty of God, people would not be called to certain vocations; others might not be experientially prepared to help others. In fact, without the trials of life, we would not have the chance to experience God at a higher level. The trials we experience are the circumstances that cause us to lean on God, build faith, and believe in the power of the Almighty.

Joseph recognized this in his life. Every trial he faced from rejection, slavery, betrayal, and, ultimately, triumph was all part of God's design. As he forgives his brothers, he makes one of the most powerful statements one could make in the aftermath of trial, "Don't be afraid. Am I in the place of God? You planned evil against me; God planned it for good to bring about the present result" (v. 19–20a). This is an amazing realization that God does not allow affliction in our lives without purpose.

When we face trials of many kinds, it is usually not because we are being punished or we have learned something more, but it's because it is a path of preparation for the will of God to take place. We are able to stand confident in the storms ahead, and the path that God leads us on because those storms along that path will lead us to eternal glory and a great commission ministry that makes disciples through personal testimony.

This story ends with an extension of compassion, kindness, and comfort. When Joseph had the opportunity to repay his brothers for every wrongdoing they did to him, his choice was to comfort them and speak kindly to them (v. 21). We can display this action when we know God is in charge. Everyone has the ability to be kind even when we are wronged, and because Joseph knew that each storm he faced in life was to bring him to the point, place, and experience he had at that moment, he knew the only option was to extend kindness.

We have the ability to know that everything works for good, more so when God has brought us through all the trials and tribulations we have faced before. The more we experience triumph through the hand of God in our trials, the more we can be confident that, no matter what storm we face, God will always be there to help us persevere. I believe this is the place where Joseph was at when he was speaking to his brothers, and we should all desire to be in the same place when we are faced with others who have wronged us.

The Hope of Our Lament

Paul's letter to the Romans reflects the persecution of the Christian church (Rom. 8:18–30). In his letter, he eloquently relays the hurt of the people through their persecution. This lament is not intended to cry about the situation but to inspire hope in the hurting church.

When we look at the passage, we can realize that our sufferings are not worth comparing with glory (v. 18). This is a perfect way to understand that, all too often, we cannot see past our current circumstance. And when we are in the midst of suffering, our vision becomes even more clouded, as I wrote previously. However, no matter the circumstance, we cannot compare it with the glory we will have in heaven. We become slaves to our circumstance, and that will prevent us from anticipating the freedom we have from those events because of eternal salvation.

Paul implies that the hope of glory draws us to salvation. Not because we seek forgiveness from a higher power, but because we seek forgiveness in order to have a relationship with God. If there were no desire for a relationship with God, what purpose would the cross serve? We accept the fact that we are sinners and in desperate need of saving because we desire relationship with the Almighty God, our sustainer. It is not because we think we might live a perfect life or because there is nothing better to do, but deep down, it is the natural desire for a relationship with our Creator.

Why would we have to? It was a hope based in something we could not see, but often we place our future in what we can see. This negates the hope of glory because we become defeated by our circumstances. Paul is instructing the reader to refocus his or her hope toward God.

God always keeps His promises. This can be found throughout the Bible and in everyday life. We have to remember though that God keeping His promises and never facing trials is two different things. God also said we would face persecution because of Christ's name (Matt. 24:9).

Because He keeps His promises, we can be patient in what God might be doing so we cherish the glory of eternity all the more. However, we often become impatient in the expectation of hope. This is not because we cannot wait to be in eternity, but because we are impatient in allowing God to lead us through our circumstances.

God is our intercessor. Most people feel stronger when they are in control, but we can only see the power of God at work in us when we are weak enough to let God take control. Many people say they have given up control over their circumstances, but in reality, they have not. Society has fooled themselves into believing this lie because that is what they want to believe. However, if you do not have a total peace over the situation, you have not given total control over to God.

God searches our hearts and knows when we surrender our circumstances to Him. When we do not know what to say or do, we do not have to say anything. That is the beauty of having the Holy Spirit in our lives. The Lord knows where we hurt. He knows when we are beat down and, most of all, knows when we are most ready to rely on Him. We just have to acknowledge the power of God over the most hidden pains we have.

The Holy Spirit gives us total peace over a situation. Through the Holy Spirit, we can reduce the anxiety of the unknown. Just as much as God searches us and we surrender ourselves to Him, God intervenes in our situation through means we might never know about. For example, when other people are involved in your trial, God can be working in their hearts just as much as He is working in yours. God does not always change the heart of the one who prays for change. He can also change the heart of everyone involved, even if not all pray for change. Resolve is not something exclusive to His people, but it is inclusive to everyone so all may see the healing power through the Holy Spirit.

Everything works for good. The healing power of the Holy Spirit allows us to know that everything that happens in our lives is for the good and glory of God. However, verse 28 gives a conditional promise that everything works for good for those who love Him (Rom. 8:28). This is an important factor because those who love God will have certain qualities that prevent them from sinning in the midst of trial or blessing.

This does not mean that God prevents good from happening to those who do not love Him. Quite the contrary, God allows good to happen for everyone. Even in the worst circumstances, God makes good from it. The issue is with whom people find the blame in the midst of the trial. For those who do not love God, they will often blame God for their circumstances. This focus is devastating because an all-loving God does allow life's trial without malice intent. In the holy perfection of Christ's death and resurrection, there is always purpose behind the trials that all people face. The new covenant promise, in my opinion, does not look at trials as punishments for sin, but looks at it as a result of sin.

Those who are facing sin issues in their lives must understand that every action reciprocates a reaction. This reaction can be positive or negative. The result is based on the continuation of the action. However, it is my belief that God does not give people cancer because they were addicted to pornography and refused to quit. I believe that people get cancer because we live in imperfect bodies.

In the same respect, imperfect bodies and minds have unhealthy desires that will draw people away from the love of God too. I am sure we have all seen the people who win the lottery and become instant millionaires. Those who chose to invest the money and go on living a normal life fare well in the sudden change of circumstance. Those who chose to change their entire lifestyle generally fall to their circumstance.

In the same respect, those who are faithful to God and choose to walk away from Him because of other desires of the heart will usually fall to their circumstances. They exchange their passion for Christ for food, money, riches, and desires of the body. When this happens the trade is for pleasures of the flesh. When issues take place in their lives, they blame their circumstances on God or poor decision making. In reality, the cause is poor decision making, just not in the immediate decision but the one that allowed them to stray away from Christ.

On the other hand, blessings are attributed to their skill and ability. For those who do not recognize God as the giver of all things, they will depend on their intellect and skillful ability to make things happen. Attributing the blessings to self or the ability to "make lemonade out of lemons," so to speak, will always draw people away from God in their lives.

This is the difference between those who recognize God's hand of protection and blessing in every circumstance and those who do not. Those who love God will always seek Him in the midst of trials and tribulation. Those who love God will always praise Him in the midst of their blessings. They will always know that, when trials are overwhelming, God will bring them through just as much as when blessings are flowing. It is at the hand of God.

The love of God gives us hope for current circumstances as well as the future. It is important for us to understand the two types of hope one can have in life. Current hope gives us the ability to know God will bring us through the circumstances based on past experiences. Future hope gives us the confidence that, regardless of our life circumstances, we are promised the glory of heaven and eternal life through Christ Jesus based in faith.

While current hope is an important promise of God that He will never leave or forsake us (Deut. 31:6; Heb. 13:5), future hope is the promise that one day there will be no more suffering (Rev. 21:4). When Paul is writing the letter to the Romans, this concept is relayed in the process of future hope (Rom. 8:30).

Paul writes of those who are called, justified, and glorified in God. Each area is important for us to understand the future hope we have in Christ. Each person is called to repentance in Christ. Each person is offered to be the heir of the throne of God (Rom. 8:17). The difference is that each person does not choose to accept the gift of salvation in order to inherit eternal life in heaven. This call to salvation is open to everyone without retribution. God does not trick people into thinking they are forgiven or even changed. When people make a full-hearted declaration for their need of Christ in their lives, they have answered the call.

Answering the call does not make life easier. In fact, it might get more difficult because we have to surrender ourselves to someone who is greater than we are. The one who is greater than we are, though, can bring us through any trial and circumstance we might face.

When I was counseling a young man who seemed to be facing multiple life-altering issues, his statement to me was, "Why can't I catch a break? Everyone else seems to have a great life, and here I am, facing work, family, financial, and personal issues." This is a common problem, but in the midst of multiple trials, we have to realize that everyone has hard times. Everyone is going to go through something bad in his or her life. Everyone will be happy, sad, frustrated, and angry at life circumstances. When we answer God's call in our lives, we have the current hope that those circumstances are only temporary.

The answered call to the arms of Christ is what justifies us in the kingdom of heaven. In the military, when we propose a change, ask for a waiver, or even request certain programming, we have to give justification. Imagine standing before judgment and hearing, "Why do you have the right to enter in the kingdom of heaven?" Some will attempt to justify why they have that right by talking about all the good stuff they have done in life, but others will simply justify themselves by knowing and being known (Gal. 4:9).

The issue is that only those who are known by God will be the ones who enter into the kingdom of heaven. Those who justify themselves will never enter, but those who are justified by Christ will enter without question. This is the future hope we have in Christ. It is the ability to say we have been called and justified in the grace of God because we know Him and He knows us.

When we answer the call, we are justified, and once this happens, we are promised to be glorified. When Jesus is praying for the believers in John 17, He says, "I have given them the glory You have given me. May they be one as We are one" (John 17:22). This glory allows us to inherit the kingdom of God. Not that we will rule it, but that we will be heirs.

With the future hope that you are from royal blood, every one of us who has the Spirit of God in us has the privilege to enter into the gates of heaven. This is the value that God holds in each person who looks to Him for hope and promise. However, we have become a world that is focused on the here and now, an earth that wants the promise fulfilled at the moment we are given it.

The kingdom of God does not work that way. Christians are not entitled to anything in this world. The blessings we receive are from God because He loves us. The trials we face are blessings from God because He is preparing us. In all things, we have the current and future hope that our purpose and call will do nothing but glorify God. This is not so that man can glorify us, but so we can be justified and enter into glory one day ourselves.

WHAT WE SHOULD USE INSTEAD

As mentioned above, suffering is a part of life. There is no way anyone will escape suffering. Status, culture, and spiritual belief will not help people avoid suffering. People overcome trials and suffering by perseverance and dependence on God. When we look at the suffering of God's people, we understand the perfection of man in Christ but also see the imperfection of man in original sin.

There was a soft knock on the hospital chaplain's office door. A saddened couple entered and had a seat. They proceeded to tell the chaplain how they had been praying over their daughter who had terminal cancer. They hurt deeply for the situation because their daughter was not getting better. The couple explained how their daughter was a devout Christian girl who loved to serve in the church and always encouraged others in prayer and the reading of God's Word.

The couple continued that they were angry with God because, despite their prayers, they were still watching their daughter suffer a horrible slow death.

"Why do bad things happen to God's people?" they asked.

This piqued the chaplain's curiosity because he had always heard it inquired, "Why do bad things happen to good people?" This was different though. We were not talking about good people anymore; we were talking about God's people.

This is different because there are several good people in the world today, but not all of them belong to God through salvation. Their questions were challenging because of their understanding of God's providence in their lives. God is supposed to protect and watch over them. God is supposed to keep all of us safe. In this case, God was allowing her to suffer a slow, horrible death, and in the end, she would die.

One thing I have found in those situations is that God will perform

His miracles in one of two ways. First, He will heal as we have prayed. Second, He will heal by taking our loved ones into heaven with Him where they will suffer no more (Rev. 21:4). This, however, does not explain why bad things happen to God's people, and after I pondered and prayed over the situation, I realized that bad things happen to God's people because of corruption of our earthly being (Rom. 7:13–24, 8:12–13; 2 Cor. 4:16–18).

First, we live in a corrupt, imperfect world. Many things on this earth can poison our minds, bodies, and souls. We are constantly being tempted to enter into corruption. The temptations lead anywhere from the sexualization of innocent products such as cologne, the glorification of drinking, as well as the genetically enhanced foods we eat.

The imperfection of the world has turned what God designed to be perfect into genetically altering the mind and body into what society has deemed perfect and acceptable. The world we live in is plagued with sinful temptations, and in the process of trying to be perfect, we have become imperfect in God's eyes.

This is not a process that has just come about as evolution of the world. We have to understand there are corrupt, imperfect people in the world as well. People who believe the worst in others, who set out to destroy others in an effort to achieve personal gain, surround us. These people are focused on themselves and only helping those within their personal circles. When we look at imperfect people, we see drug dealers, murderers, thieves, and prostitutes. These people have perverted a social setting that draws others into distress and trials.

That is not to say that corrupt, imperfect people are not all around us. We have all sinned and come short of God's glory (Rom. 3:23). Because we are all sinners in need of God's grace, we come to understand that we are part of the corrupt, imperfect world. The difference between those who have Christ in their lives and those who do not is their view between right and wrong. However, if you slander your coworker's reputation or you gossip about your neighbors, is your need for salvation less than that of the drug dealer or sexually impure person? The answer is no.

We are all in the same need of salvation, and we are all entrapped by the desire to sin. When Christ is in our lives, our spirits are made new, and our actions are revealed through the counsel of the Holy Spirit. As well, Christians are held to a different standard than those who have not heard the gospel. Once we hear the truth of our behavior, we are held accountable to our actions.

This is the concept of being blind to sin. I often ask others, "How can you hold a child accountable for taking a cookie from the cookie jar when he did not know he was not allowed? But when the child has been told not to, he is accountable to his decision of right and wrong." The imperfection of people is not that they do not know what social law is. They do not know what spiritual law is.

Just as we are all imperfect people, we all live in corrupt, imperfect bodies (2 Cor. 4:16). Regardless of the renewing of our spirits, we all live with failing and ailing bodies. No matter how hard we try to be healthy, skinny, or muscular or have the perfect profile, our bodies are imperfect. Disease, sickness, and desire corrupt them. While there are great advances in modern medical care, nothing can prevent the imperfection of our bodies from failing at some point. In other words, all our bodies die.

When I was young in the army, I could run my two-mile fitness test in ten and a half minutes, or at least that is the fastest time I clocked. While at my first duty station, I injured my Achilles tendon. After I recovered from that injury, the fastest I could run my two-mile fitness test was fourteen minutes and forty-five seconds. This was a damaging blow to my twentysomething-year-old body. However, it goes to show just how frail and fragile the body is.

No matter what kind of shape you are in, we are all susceptible to disease. I have seen time and time again that people who seemed to be the picture of health fall to devastating illness. This was not because God cursed them with it. Our spirits are the only things that are made perfect in Christ.

So often, we expect that Christ will perfect our bodies, the people around us, and the world, but that is not what perfects a Christian. The Holy Spirit within them perfects their spirit and helps them make the right choices. Bad things are always going to happen to God's people because of the corrupt imperfection we live in. It does not mean that God has left our side or we even go through these trials because God is mad. It means that He will bring us through, one way or another.

Saying that all things happen for good is not a lie when we look at future hope. In the immediate though, it can be frustrating because we want the good. As believers and people who counsel loved ones and friends through difficult times, what we need to provide is peace in their lives.

PEACE

Peace is not only an overwhelming feeling of comfort, but it serves a purpose. As God's helping agent to a hurting world, the way we should bring peace to someone's life is through the acronym PEACE.

- Prepare Us
- Experience
- Audit Self
- Closer to Him
- Endurance

Looking at each of the words, we find encouragement that will help us get through the difficult time and transition into understanding the blessing and intent God had by allowing us to go through the trial.

The trials in our lives *prepare us* for anything we might face in the future. In James 1, we learn that we go through the trials of life so "you may be mature and complete, lacking nothing" (James 1:4b). This speaks to the joy that trials will bring in life. The trials will produce endurance, and as it does its complete work, you will lack nothing. Each trial we face will prepare us for the challenges of God's call in our lives. Even when we make bad decisions in our lives, God will use those decisions to prepare us for what is ahead.

Experience prepares us for God's call in our lives. Luke chronicles the ministry of Paul, and as Barnabas and he return to Antioch from Syria, they encouraged the disciples by saying, "We must go through many hardships to enter the kingdom of God" (Acts 14:22). These hardships were referring to the teaching of Christ in the book of John. Christ teaches that we will go through hardships because of our relationship with Him (John 15:20, 16:33). We have to remember that God desires to have relationship with His creation, just like a dad desires to have a relationship with his teenage son. However, just like the world tempts the teenage son away from his father, things of the world easily tempt us away from God.

When we gain experience in the trials we face, we are better witnesses to the healing hand of God. There is no better testimony to hope than the evidence of those who have faced and overcome trials in their life. We can have peace knowing that each experience, good or bad, is designed to encourage us, reaffirm hope, and grow in our understanding of who God is in our lives.

When facing a trial in life, an *audit of yourself* is one of the most important aspects to getting through a trial. Seek God and ask Him to reveal what you would learn from the situation. When we are able to look within, we learn a great deal about ourselves. Why do we handle issues the way we do? What makes us angry at some things but not at others? These are all questions that we can ask. One of the greatest ways to find or help guide others toward peace in life is to help them look deep within. When you look within yourself, you can ask some questions that might help get you moving in the right direction:

- Why do I feel overwhelmed in this situation?
- How is this situation going to change my life for the positive?
- How does God play a role in getting me through this situation?
- Have I really surrendered the situation to God?
- If I have really surrendered the situation, how do I depend on God from this point forward?
- Where is my heart in this situation? Am I focused on glorifying God or revenge?

These are only a few questions that can be asked when facing your own heart. I am sure you can probably think of a few more inquiries that are personal and applicable to the situation you might be facing. Regardless the situation, it is always good for people to examine their lives and know their hearts are in the right place to glorify God and live by his standards.

When we examine our lives, we automatically draw *closer to Him*. We begin to see purpose in the storm. We understand the reasoning behind our situation. Though we might not be able to see the entire picture of what the situation will bring, we sharpen our focus to see how God will bring us through the current sight picture. In the same respect, we find strength in God when we are weakest (2 Cor. 12:9–10). This is the peace that we can find in the midst of drawing closer to God. The closer we are to God, the more we will see through the lenses of the Holy Spirit. The less we try to take control of situations, the more we allow the Holy Spirit to take control of the situation.

The best time to draw close to God is not in the middle of our trials, but before the trial starts. I know an army soldier who would pray before every mission. He used to tell his troops that the best time to pray was not when the bullets started to fly, but before the mission started. When the bullets started to fly, you have to focus on the mission and be close enough to God to know His strength will overcome your fear.

We have to remember that, every morning we wake up, we are in premission mode. Satan can attack us on the way to work or as we get the kids ready for school or talk to our coworkers. And the list goes on. We are vulnerable to Satan's attack at any time. The best time to run for God is not in that attack, but before the mission starts.

The challenge is to draw close to God from the moment you wake so, when the evil one attacks you, you are drawing on the strength and protection of God. Then you are able to find joy in the affliction because you will have a front-row seat to seeing the powerful hand of God at work in your life, as well as the person or situation you might be facing.

When we are able to see the powerful hand of God at work in our lives, we endure all things. *Endurance* allows us to weather the storms of life. As Paul writes in Romans, endurance gives us character and hope (Rom. 5:1–5).

Shortly after my Achilles injury, I had difficulty keeping pace in formation runs. It was common for me to fall out of a run as I tried to rebuild endurance in my legs. This was difficult and discouraging for me because I never used to have issues running. After falling out of a few formation runs, my platoon leader made me cut a heart out of manila folder paper, laminate it, and carry it with me everywhere I went.

His thought was that the heart would remind me to endure the pain of recovery so my character would show leadership and inspire hope in my life. Every time I was asked to show heart in a situation, I would have to pull out the heart and show I had the endurance, character, and hope to fully recover from my injury.

Ultimately I recovered from my injury and passed off the heart to another person in my platoon. When we face trials in our lives, we have to reach into our spiritual dependence on God, who reminds us that we can and will endure the trials of life. Going through the issues we face is how we build character in our lives. They are the battle scars that remind us hope is found in all situation because God will bring us through or call us home. Either way, we have the hope of Christ on our side. There is no other reason to endure the hardships of life and make them worth living without the current or future hope of Christ in our lives.

The concept of PEACE draws us closer to God and gives us strength to face the situation. When we resolve in our hearts that we will not seek revenge, we receive a freedom from the burden, which gives us peace. In turn we become emotionally stable and better caretakers for those God entrusts us to disciple and lead in life.

In our lives, when trials and tribulation come our way, it is up to us to find the hope that only comes from the peace that passes all understanding. This is the only way to weather the storm without significant damage to our spirits. Drawing closer to God now only makes us stronger when the storms of life come our way.

CHAPTER 6

SELF-REFLECTION OR SMALL GROUP DISCUSSION QUESTIONS

1. Have you ever faced an issue in life where you were not able to see God's purpose or goodness in? What happened?

2. What times have you allowed fear to overcome your circumstances?

3. How does the sovereignty of God play a role in your life?

4. When faced with opposition in life, how do you react to difficult situations? Does guilt, revenge, and judgment show, or is it kindness, compassion, and comfort?

5. How does kindness, compassion, and comfort become the characteristics when people bring affliction in our lives?

6. What ways do you display hope in your life? Include future and current.

7. How does corruption and imperfection affect your life and shape the way you react to difficult situations?

8. How can you use the acronym PEACE to get through various trials in your life? How can you use it to help others get through their trials in life?

9. In what ways can you draw closer to God in your life?

10. What changes do you need to make in life so you can weather the storm better?

SESSION 8: WRAPPING IT UP

The Cross of Christ bears the suffering and the sin of mankind, including our own. Jesus accepts all this with open arms...

—Pope Francis

It is not up to us, but to God who speaks through the Bible. We tend to forget that in this day and age. One of my seminary professors said, with the development of the Internet, you could always find reference material to back your belief, right or wrong. The unfortunate part about that is that you can always find a sermon, pastor, or counselor who manipulates the Bible in a way that allows him or her to share his or her theology of God, right or wrong.

When this happens, people will mislead others into believing falsehoods about who God is in their lives and, worse, end up missing opportunity for salvation because they might have been told a good life led is a life good enough to get into heaven. What they have missed is that we in no way can enter the kingdom of heaven by the life we lead. It is only through Jesus Christ. This myth sounds good and makes us feel good about ourselves, but in the end, scripture tells us Jesus is "the way, the truth, and the life." No man shall go to God but through him (John 14:6).

This means we cannot get to heaven by feeding the homeless or donating clothes to the poor. We can only receive eternal life by having a relationship with God. If we make any other attempt, we are missing the vital part of God's plan for salvation. If you believed that being a good person would be your ticket into heaven, you have taken salvation into your own hands and determined that Christ's work on the cross is irrelevant to eternal security.

This thought might upset people because they believe they have placed their trust in Jesus, but they have only placed their trust in their ability to receive salvation through earning their place in heaven. We have to remember we cannot buy our way into heaven when the gift of salvation is given freely. We are not enslaved by the hand of God as a bond for our sinful nature, but we are set free through the blood of Christ through His perfect nature.

SUFFERING FOR JESUS IN THE FALL OF MAN

Too many Christians walk around as if they are sad and depressed that they have to follow the scriptures and do what the Bible tells them. As sarcastically as they can put it, they are "suffering for Jesus." We have it backward though. We should not suffer to have or even maintain a relationship with Jesus, but we should be reminded that Jesus suffered so he could have and maintain a relationship with us.

God's desire to have relationship with us is so great that He chose to suffer in order to restore what He once had with His creation. Suffering in this world is not because God makes us do it, but because Satan wants to take the relationship with God away from us. Think about it. If God wants a relationship with us so badly that He would give His only begotten son (John 3:16) in order to bridge the gap of sin and death, why would Satan want to allow it?

It is all based on our understanding of Lucifer's fall from heaven. In the book of Ezekiel, we learn that Lucifer was a bright and beautiful angel with all the splendor of a star. He was held in the highest regard and authority in the heavens (Ezek. 28:11–18). However, Lucifer attempted to rise to the highest parts of the heavens because of his desire to take God's position in the world (Isa. 14:12–15). God recognized his mutinous behavior and cast him to the deepest regions of hell.

This is only the beginning. Lucifer fell because of his desire for power and presence over God. We know this had to have happened before Adam and Eve ate from the tree because the tempter was in the garden. This is the first sign that following people outside of God is wrong. When the people around us only have intention for their own desire, power, popularity, and authority, they are not in line with God's will for their lives.

When I was working in a small church, a pastor always said, "Follow me as long as I am following God." While this makes sense, it does not hold a good theological stance. We are not called to follow people; we are called to follow Christ. As long as Christ is in the church, we can participate in the ministry of Christ through the church.

Satan wants us to follow him. His desire is to tempt us with seemingly harmless aspects to our lives in a way that will pull us away from our relationship with God. God banished Satan for his actions, and we can understand that being away from God is being banished from heaven and doomed to hell (Luke 10:18; Rev. 9:1). Just as Satan fell from heaven because he attempted to take control of things, we too fall from heaven when we delete God from our lives in order to pursue our heart's desires outside of God.

When Lucifer fell from the heavens, he took a large number of the angels with him (Rev. 12:3–9). Through false teaching, manipulation, and personal desire for power, he was able to convince people to leave. These angels, I am sure, believed that Lucifer was in the right because of the way he communicated why he should be in charge.

We know Satan can convince us to sin in many situations because Adam and Eve were tempted to sin from the tree of knowledge (Gen. 3). This also shows us Satan's initial desire to take us away from God, no matter how strong our relationship is. He does this by manipulating the truth, telling us things mean something different than what God intends for our lives. It is the false teachings of people who might sound good and have eloquent speech, the ones that believe, if we feel good about ourselves, we do not need to address the sin in our lives that pull us away from God.

We find people all over that say things that can appear to draw us closer to God, but in reality, they take away from the truths that give us freedom in God. After Adam and Eve ate from the tree, what they believed would make them free bound them and limited their abilities to function in the freedom of the garden and with God. In the same respect, God desires for us to have freedom in and with Him, but our sin limits and binds us to operate in that freedom.

This devastation takes us away from God. Satan's number-one goal is to devour our lives so much that we feel there is no chance of recovery (1

Peter 5:8). In everything we do, we have to be wise, loving, and kind. These characteristics allow us to know we are following the truth of scripture.

Unlike many people, faiths, and belief systems, the one confidence we have is that Satan loses in the end (Rev. 20:3). Satan can draw us away from God, but in the end-times, Satan will be bound, and all those who strayed away from God, followed the lies, and discipled people outside of God's truth will be bound up with him in the pits of hell.

I do not say this as doom and gloom, but as a reality that Christians who love and follow truth will remain in the Lord while those who were led astray do not hear His voice because they do not belong to Him (John 10:27–28). We have to be discerning enough to recognize, hear, and heed the voice of God.

No Crisis Is the Same

Pithy statements will not give people peace. The Holy Spirit provides hope in the midst of trials. As believers and helping agents for those in the midst of life's trials, we serve as the conduit in which the Holy Spirit provides that hope. We have to make ourselves available, surrender our own knowledge, and seek God for the wisdom to help guide people to the peace they desire. Statements and methods that work for one person might not work for another. Because of this, using the same thing repetitively can become ineffective.

One time as a clinical intern, I prayed with a couple who had just lost their baby. The prayer I said really helped the couple, and in the end, they both commented on the peace they felt through the imagery spoken. I remember thinking about what I had prayed and attempted to work some of the effective statements into other similar prayers. As a result, the prayers were not as impactful, because I was reciting something that worked for one person but might not have been meant for others.

We have to remember that the Holy Spirit will always guide us in the words, deeds, and direction we should move in our lives. When prayers and statements are recited with the expectation they will work as a blanket hope for others, they become empty and meaningless. Eventually they carry no empathy or emotion toward the other person's situation. It is our job as believers to help guide people toward hope in the Lord, not provide cliché statements that might make us feel better but do little for those we are trying to help.

An Awesome Responsibility

Some people will take on the responsibility to share truth in a way that might create criticism from their friends and family. Pastors will stand behind the pulpit and preach truth despite the size of their congregation, and Christians all around the world will share the gospel message in truth and love at the cost of many friendships. This is the responsibility we have as believers.

Some people claim they have taken on that responsibility, but in reality, they will only take up their cross to the point of losing friends, family, congregants, or status. Once the challenge is put forth, they will falter at the fear of the unknown. We have to remember that "faith is the reality of what is hoped for, the proof of what is not seen" (Heb. 11:1). Those who are worried more about their worldly needs being met lack the faith of current and future hope as discussed previously.

Jesus said that if we love our father, mother, son, or daughter more than Him, we are not worthy of Him (Matt. 10:37). We are to first take up our cross and follow Christ. It does not mean that we hate everyone in our family, but it means we love Christ first and foremost in our lives. When we love God, we will show love toward the people in our families.

When I was in middle school, I was very devout in my faith. As I have said previously, my family was in church anytime the doors were open. A boy in the school would always tempt me into various inappropriate behaviors. As I consistently denied his temptations, he finally screamed down the crowded middle school hallway, "Come on, Jesus freak. Turn the other cheek as I beat you in the ground."

I remember running down the hall toward him, full of anger and ready to fight. I got up in his face with my fists clinched, and as I was ready to speak, the only thing that came out was "You're right. I love Jesus, but that doesn't mean I won't kick your ..." Well, you get it.

He was surprised at my action and quickly backed down, but in a hall full of preteen kids ready to see a fight, something in me told me that would be a defining moment in my life, and it was. I was made fun of for my faith. I was ridiculed for who and what I claimed to be, and ultimately I ran away from the church as fast as I could. I loved anything but the authority of my parents and my God in order to please the people around me.

It was thirteen years I strayed on that path, but something would always draw me toward the ethical decision making based in my early childhood understanding of the Bible. Then a moment came that I was once again redefined. I realized I did not have to impress the world with my ability to drink or reject God. I realized I needed to serve God with truth, one that exclaimed my love for Jesus and thus my passion to serve God.

Some might be reading this book and think they are ready to give up on the hypocrisy that can be found in some churches today. We have to remember, though, this is Satan's way of drawing you away from the community of believers because it is easier to attack the lone sheep than it is to attack the herd.

Never let your frustration with an imperfect world, people, or body draw you away from God. Never let the rejection of friends and family who think you might have become one of those crazy religious zealots keep you from loving and serving God in truth. Most of all, never let someone who claims to speak the Word of God with confidence make you believe that contradicting the Bible is okay. The truth of God's Word is timeless and infallible, applicable to every generation, situation, and culture.

It is our responsibility to develop a relationship with God so we no longer misuse the Bible in order to make ourselves feel better. More so, we are to use it in order to change our lives as well as the lives of those around us. As you finish this book, use the truth of God's Word to grow and disciple others. Show them the love and light of the Holy Spirit. Through this love and light, they will gain peace and comfort in the arms of the Lord.

CHAPTER 7

SELF-REFLECTION OR SMALL GROUP DISCUSSION QUESTIONS

1. Have you ever been misled by the teachings of a pastor, counselor, or religious leader?

2. How have you detected or overcome the false teachings of others?

3. Have you ever made a statement that worked in one situation so you used it in many because you thought it was successful? What happened?

4. How do you see Satan attempting to take away from your relationship with Christ?

5. When was a time you downplayed another person's crisis because you did not believe it was a big issue?

6. Has anyone every downplayed your personal crisis? How did that make you feel?

7. How has this book helped you understand your responsibility to the truth of God's Word?

8. How has this book helped you grow in your understanding of encouraging others?

9. What things in your life will you change as a result of reading this book and the emphasis on pursuing truth?

Printed in the United States
By Bookmasters